TEEN FATHERS

TEEN FATHERS

PAUL LANG AND SUSAN S. LANG

THE CHANGING FAMILY
FRANKLIN WATTS
NEW YORK•CHICAGO•LONDON•TORONTO•SYDNEY

Library of Congress Cataloging-in-Publication Data

Lang, Paul (Paul C.)
Teen Fathers / Paul Lang and Susan S. Lang.
p. cm. — (The Changing family)
Includes bibliographical references and index.
Summary: Discusses issues related to teenage fatherhood, including
costs to children and society, strategies for coping, acknowledging
paternity, and minority fathers. Includes resource list of organizations,
books, articles, and videotapes.
ISBN 0-531-11216-0 (lib. bdg.)
1. Teenage fathers—United States—Juvenile literature.
[1. Teenage fathers.] I. Lang, Susan S. II. Title. III. Series: Changing
family (New York, N.Y.)
HQ756.7.L36 1995
306.85'6—dc20   95-1349
                                                                                 CIP AC

Dedicated to our father,
Solon J. Lang

CONTENTS

ACKNOWLEDGMENTS

We would like to thank, most of all, the young fathers and their relatives who agreed to be interviewed for this book. Their names (sometimes changed) and their ideas appear here often and the book could not have been written without their contributions.

Dozens of professionals who work with teenage parents were also generous with their time and insights. Special debts of gratitude go to the following:

Jeannette Abell: GRADS (Graduation, Reality and Dual-Role Skills) teacher, Kent Roosevelt and Hudson High Schools in Ohio;

William Allen: former graduate student at the University of Minnesota and author of *Being There* (1992), his master's thesis on young black fathers;

Liz Araujo: Girls Inc., in Lynn, Massachusetts;

Thomas Braun: Society for the Prevention of Cruelty to Children, in Salem, Massachusetts;

Betty Cook and Elaine McClay: Teen Advocate Program, in Baton Rouge, Louisiana;

Sharon Enright: Ohio Department of Education and National Diffusion Network;

Daniel B. Frank: (formerly) Our Place, in Evanston, Illinois, and author of *Deep Blue Funk* (1983);

Delores Holmes: Family Focus (Our Place), in Evanston, Illinois;

Linnea Johnson-Scott: (formerly) Office of Support Enforcement, in Olympia, Washington;

John Lass: INSIGHTS Teen Parent Program, in Portland, Oregon;

Dr. Melvin Moore: Youth and Family Center and EKO Multi-Purpose Center, in Inglewood and Compton, California;

Juan Munoz: (formerly) Reaching Out to Chelsea Adolescents (ROCA), in Chelsea, Massachusetts;

Dick Muzzey: Catholic Charities, in Lynn, Massachusetts;

David Perez: Society for the Prevention of Cruelty to Children, in Lawrence, Massachusetts;

Ron Poindexter: (formerly) Urban League, in Roxbury, Massachusetts; and

Bernadine Watson, Public/Private Ventures, in Philadelphia;

Ed Woodley: (formerly) The Bridge Program, in Seattle.

Bryan E. Robinson, author of *Teenage Fathers* and other works on the subject, appears more often than any other writer in the notes to this book and we are happy to acknowledge how often we followed where he led.

Finally, thanks to our family for its encouragement and support. Our niece, fifteen-year-old Sarah Lang, proved to be a shrewd critic and we are grateful for her advice.

Paul Lang
Susan S. Lang

TEEN FATHERS

THE STORIES OF TWO DIFFERENT TEEN FATHERS

There are young fathers who choose not to take on the responsibilities of fatherhood, often because of their immaturity, and there are teen fathers who welcome the responsibility.

I. WHEN TEEN FATHERS WALK AWAY: DANIEL'S STORY

Daniel, who is twenty years old, but looks—and acts—a lot younger, has abandoned his child. His family came to the United States from Central America when Daniel was about ten. His English is good and he attended high school until his sophomore year, when he was thrown out for drinking. Daniel, who has also been involved with drugs, went to a few high school equivalency (GED) classes, but then dropped them.

His girlfriend, whom he had known for several years, became pregnant when they both were eighteen. She wanted to get an abortion or give the child up for adoption, but Daniel talked her out of it and promised to get a job that would support them all. Daniel says, however, that he was turned off by the way his girlfriend started to look as she got heavier during the last months of the pregnancy. That may have hurt their relationship.

After the child was born, Daniel did get a factory job, but he lost it because, as he admits, he often got to work late since he likes staying up at night and watching TV.

"I don't really take care of the baby much," admits Daniel. "I never change the diaper. Maybe I've fed her a couple of times, but I don't feel that close to her because she's a girl. And me and the mother don't get along anymore."

Daniel claims he has stopped drinking and taking drugs and has been looking for another job, but now he's gotten another girl pregnant. The mother of his first child doesn't know yet about his second girlfriend's pregnancy.

"I never used protection with my second girlfriend," Daniel explains, "because I don't like how condoms feel."

He looks a little ashamed. He knows that isn't the whole story.

With a sheepish smile, he adds, "Really, I guess I wanted her to get pregnant, so I can leave the girl I'm living with now. We'll see! If it's a boy, I'll marry her [the second girlfriend], but if she doesn't have a boy. . . . Well, I don't know if I would stick around with her. I like her a lot, though."

Daniel is a likable person, and he doesn't try to pretend that the decisions he's made have all been good ones. He has tried to improve himself: GED classes, his factory job, stopping the drinking and drugs, looking for a new job. But by almost anyone's standards he isn't a good father or much help to the girlfriends he's gotten pregnant.

Daniel resented that his first girlfriend put on weight during her pregnancy, although she was carrying HIS baby. And if the second girlfriend has a daughter, he is ready to abandon both young women and leave them to take care of his children themselves. Perhaps he may yet grow out of the immature attitudes that put his own comfort and satisfaction so far ahead of the welfare of his children and their mothers.

II. HOW SOCIETY CAN WORK AGAINST TEEN FATHERS: STEPHEN'S STORY

Some teenage dads want to be full-time, committed fathers, but society makes it hard for them. Take Stephen, a teenager who had to fight the system just to keep custody with his wife, Lisa, of their son, Stephen Anthony.

FROM THE TOP OF THE WORLD . . .
TO A PUBLIC SHELTER

Stephen can remember watching the birth of his child in the hospital and how happy and relieved he and the baby's mother, Lisa, were that their son was healthy. Yet the three years since their son was born have been the most painful of his life, he says, even though he and Lisa had planned the pregnancy and were delighted to be the parents of little Stephen Anthony.

"Fighting the system almost finished us," the young father says.

Stephen is a tall, soft-spoken 22-year-old Irish-American. His mother is alive, but his stepfather died two years ago. The only time Stephen sounds angry is when he talks about the last time he saw his own father, a man who had left home the day Stephen was born and never came back.

"I was ten years old the last time I saw him. He was drunk in a bar. He gave me twenty bucks and I never saw him again. When people ask me about him, I say he's dead." When Stephen talks about "fighting the system" along with Lisa to keep their little family together his voice is bitter:

> *I was working as a tow truck driver three years ago. Lisa and I weren't married yet, but I was making good money and we started trying to have a baby.*
>
> *I had just begun my shift, it was about 12:30 in the morning, when Lisa called to say she was pregnant. We were so excited and happy.*
>
> *But just before the time Lisa was due, everything fell apart.*
>
> *Two cars rammed into the back of the tow truck I was on. I slipped two disks in my back and fractured part of the backbone in my neck. I haven't been able to work since.*
>
> *And at just the same time, we got thrown out of our apartment. I've been working since I was thirteen, but I knew we had to get some help.*
>
> *When we went to the welfare office after we'd gotten the eviction notice, their line was, "Call us when you're out on the street. Then we can help you." We kept calling around: the mayor, the governor's office, anyone we could think of. All we got was the runaround.*

*And they were telling us at the hospital that
if we didn't have a place to live after the baby
was born, they were going to take him away!*

Luckily, the young couple and their newborn were able to move into a small apartment in another town, where they lived with Lisa's sister and three other relatives. But there were still enormous problems. Lisa and Stephen both wanted to get their high school equivalency (GED) diplomas and Stephen had to wait for the settlement check from his accident. Losing fights with the Welfare Department seemed to take up all their energy. Eventually, they had to move out of the sister's apartment, first into a motel and finally, when all their savings were gone, into a public shelter.

Stephen thinks that the problems the couple has faced have brought them closer together. He admits, however, that at times he wanted to leave his wife and son and just see Stephen Anthony now and then, because he knew that government agencies were more generous to young mothers on their own than toward young couples.

"Lisa told me she wanted me to stay," he remembers with a smile. "She didn't *want* to be left alone and we still loved each other."

Although they finally got money together for an apartment in a new city, the couple had almost given up any hope of getting their GEDs. They could barely make the rent.

A PROGRAM FOR TEEN PARENTS
LENDS A HAND

Stephen feels lucky that about this time he and Lisa connected with a program for young mothers in Chelsea,

17

Massachusetts, a city just outside Boston with high unemployment and an active gang population. Reaching Out to Chelsea Adolescents (ROCA) used its small budget to provide services that address the everyday problems of teenage mothers—day care, GED preparation, job training, caring for their babies. The staff also helped with the paperwork needed for the agencies that provide welfare checks, public housing, food stamps, and payment of medical bills.

As luck would have it, Stephen found that Juan Munoz, then a counselor at ROCA, was starting a group to address the needs of young *fathers*, to teach them skills as well as encourage them to get their lives in order to be good fathers to their children. During the two years Lisa and Stephen have been involved with ROCA, they have been able to get day care and welfare assistance. Both earned GEDs and Lisa has trained as a medical assistant. Stephen has been trying to get the money together to go back to school in electronics.

Stephen speaks proudly about how he and Lisa share the duties—and pleasures—of taking care of Stephen Anthony. He's proud, too, about Lisa's future career, but with only one month's work experience, Lisa hasn't been able to find a job in her field and she's starting to get discouraged.

"I'm afraid we may be going downhill again," she says.

Not that they've lost hope by any means. Stephen thinks one thing that has kept up his spirits has been talking about his problems, and hearing how other teenagers are coping, in frequent "young fathers' breakfasts" held on Saturday mornings at ROCA. The fathers often bring their children along. Talking with Juan Munoz and a half-dozen other young dads after an eggs-and-sausage breakfast, Stephen said he hoped the worst of his problems was over.

"It isn't that teens make bad parents," he says. "Society makes it impossible for them to be good ones. I just know I'll do anything it takes so my son doesn't have to go it alone without a real dad, like I did."

HOW TYPICAL IS
STEPHEN'S STORY?

Stephen's story is one of extremes — from hope to hardship to hope again. It shows, however, that even when a young father has a lot going for him, the system may work against him.

Stephen's resentment at not having had a father he could count on while growing up is shared by a lot of young people. Many people in need, as were Stephen and Lisa, are exhausted from fighting government agencies that are supposed to help them. Government welfare programs give many young fathers the message that they might be doing the mother and baby a favor by leaving.

Yet Stephen, Lisa and Stephen Anthony, unlike many very young families, have a lot going for them:

• Stephen and Lisa were both in their late teens and wanted a baby when Stephen Anthony was born.

Unwanted children of very young teenagers often do not grow up in a good environment. The parents' lack of money is only one reason. Couples in their early and middle teens often can't deal with the problems between them *and* at the same time give the baby their full attention. Most of these couples break up after a short time.

> • Stephen and Lisa were already a committed couple when she became pregnant. Stephen was involved in the preparations for the birth and he was at Lisa's side in the hospital. Both parents take care of their baby.

Many teenage mothers have to "go it alone" if the father of their baby doesn't remain with them. Even some young fathers who take responsibility for their child don't get involved in everyday tasks like feeding and changing the baby.

> • Lisa's family gave the couple help when they needed it most. Both Stephen and Lisa also found good advice as well as friends among the other young families at a community center near their town.

Even in fairly small communities, programs for teenage mothers can be located through such groups as the YWCA, the Urban League, and the Society for the Prevention of Cruelty to Children. If teenage fathers get the feeling that they're not welcome to participate with the mothers in these programs, they should insist that they be allowed to participate.

> • Stephen and Lisa both obtained high school equivalency diplomas, and Lisa has even earned a certificate as a medical assistant.

It is very common for teenage mothers and fathers to drop out of school and never to return to their education. They often find themselves in low-paying jobs and one or both may have to work two or even three part-time jobs to make ends meet. However, education programs designed for teenage parents of both sexes can enhance the difference to the well-being of the parents and the child.

Even when the teenage father and mother do everything they can to bring up their baby right, sometimes the social service departments that are set up to aid can actually help drive the couple apart. The young couple must find support within their families or in some community organization that can reach out to them—to both the father and mother.

A 1989 study showed that only *one in six* of the teens who fathered children with adolescent mothers lived with their children.[1] Almost two out of three of the adolescent mothers in the study reported that the fathers provided too little—or no—financial support to the mother and child.[2]

The lack of financial commitment from the father often indicates that he does not have any strong sense of responsibility for his child. But the one to pay the highest price when a young father walks away is the baby he abandons.

YOUNG FATHERS AND THEIR BABIES

Teenagers are given a double message from society. They watch movies and TV shows and listen to love songs that all show romance as the best part of being young. Yet, schools and parents disapprove of their experimenting with sex until they're older.

SEX EDUCATION

Schools provide sex education, but these programs often simply emphasize the ideal of abstinence (not having sex), and never get around to informing students how to avoid a pregnancy if they are sexually active. Not even the rise of sexually transmitted diseases, including AIDS, among young people has changed the emphasis on self-control as the way to avoid pregnancy and prevent the spread of disease.

Many parents and community and religious leaders believe that discussing birth control in any detail tells students that having sex is all right as long as precautions are taken. These adults are even more disturbed at the

23

suggestion that a school nurse might distribute condoms or other birth-control devices without the parents ever giving their consent or being informed.

If birth-control information is not provided by parents or teachers, teenagers may believe the stories they hear from their friends—who may not know what they're talking about. Many young people don't believe that teenagers as young as thirteen or fourteen years old can get pregnant. Or they think girls don't get pregnant unless they have sex dozens of times. Some understand that pregnancy is less likely on certain days of a girl's menstrual cycle, but they don't calculate which days correctly. Others, of course, just don't think about pregnancy when they are in the heat of passion.

Although one study found that almost nine out of ten teenagers who were having sex knew where to get contraceptives, only about *one in ten* used birth control even occasionally.[1]

Some teens don't use birth control because their sexual partners talk them out of it. Over half the boys in one study said their girlfriends resisted using contraceptives and over 20 percent of the girls who used no protection told researchers the reason was that "my boyfriend didn't want me to use it."[2]

Teenagers often have confused feelings about using birth control. One teenage girl who was sleeping with her boyfriend visited her doctor to find out if she was pregnant. When she was asked if she and her boyfriend were using contraception, she answered, "I don't know if I'd feel right taking [birth control pills]. You shouldn't use them if you're not married. . . . The way I see it, if I use birth control, that makes me a bad girl. If I don't use anything, even if I get pregnant, I'm a good girl who got caught."[3]

Many teenage boys think it's their girlfriend's fault if she gets pregnant. One young man reacted with anger after he found out his girlfriend was expecting their baby. Even though they had been having intercourse for months and never discussed birth control, he felt she had tricked him: "I thought you [were] taking care of yourself. I thought you went and got pills and everything. I just *assumed*."[4] Birth control was the girl's responsibility as far as this teenager was concerned and her pregnancy seemed like her way of manipulating him unfairly.

Teenagers of both sexes are *equally* responsible for making sure that they don't produce a child together that they will not be able to take care of. Sexual abstinence is the surest way of doing this. But teenagers also need to know how to get and use birth control if they do not abstain but instead have sex. Blaming each other after a child has been conceived is not going to make the problem go away.

Some teachers and social service workers are trying to convince teenagers to put off having sex until they're married, or at least until they're older. As *one part* of an overall sex education program, such an approach can sometimes get across an important message, one that if believed could reduce the number of children with teenage parents, namely: "Virginity is not a dirty word."

PROMOTING ABSTINENCE AMONG
TEENAGE MALES

One factor that has complicated the lives of all sexually active Americans has been the threat of contracting sexually transmitted diseases, especially AIDS. "AIDS has become the greatest threat to teenagers," says Daniel B. Frank, the author of *Deep Blue Funk & Other Stories: Portraits of Teenage Parents.* "The issue isn't so much whether kids are getting pregnant or not anymore," says Frank, now head of the Francis Parker School, in Chicago. "Now the issue is whether they will survive their teenage years without becoming infected with a fatal disease. Having a baby pales in importance next to the threat of AIDS."

In fact, the spread of AIDS to the teenage population—heterosexual as well as homosexual—is leading some schools to introduce sex education to students even before they reach their teens, usually emphasizing abstinence. Also, more and more school nurses are distributing condoms to teenage students who ask for them. But there has been enormous resistance to many of these programs from parents and others who don't want schools "encouraging" sex by teaching children about contraception and by giving out condoms to teenagers, especially without the parents' consent. Part of the resistance to sex-education programs comes from the picture of teenagers (especially teenage males) as completely irresponsible. The idea is that given a little information about sexuality, the boys will be even more eager to have sex—with or without a condom—and then will leave the girl to deal with her pregnancy alone.

There have been some programs that try to "sell" the idea of abstinence to teenagers. In a statewide campaign in Maryland that began in 1987, classroom talks to students, billboards, posters, and television commercials were used to try to convince teenagers to put off having sex. One poster directed at teenage males shows an unhappy young man holding an infant in his arms. "A baby costs $474 a month. How much do you have in your pocket?"[5] The advertising campaign also includes sponsoring talks on abstinence by local coaches and other adult men in the community and displaying billboards with the slogan "[Virginity Is] Not a Dirty Word." *The New York Times* reported in January 1994 that the entire $5 million campaign was credited with reducing teenage pregnancy in the state by 10 percent over two years.[6]

Dajahn Blevins, a health educator with the Urban League in San Diego, believes that teenagers will change their sexual behavior if they can see some practical reasons to do so. For the teenage males, these reasons range from the fact that a condom will prevent lice ("crabs"), herpes, or genital warts to the realization that lunch money won't go very far in buying Pampers or baby formula.

"We tell [the teenagers that] the opportunity to get an education can pass you by," Blevins explains, "but the opportunity to have sex ain't going nowhere." But Blevins and the other workers in the program don't "preach" abstinence. "We don't tell kids never to have sex," he says. Instead, he tries to convince them that they need to make something of themselves and that becoming menaces instead of contributors to society is selling out. "And kids hate to sell out," he adds.[7]

But even many health educators who believe fervently in the medical, psychological, moral, and spiritual advantages of abstinence for teenagers feel comfortable providing birth-control information to teenagers who are sexually active. Jeannette Abell has been a teacher with the GRADS (*G*raduation, *R*eality *A*nd *D*ual-role *S*kills) program, in Ohio, for ten years and many of her students

27

have been young fathers. Ideally, she hopes they will change their ways and realize they are too young to be having sex.

However, the fifty-year-old mother of three realizes that ideals and reality don't always match. "I don't have a problem with giving them information on [birth control] devices," she explains. "They have to know how to prevent further pregnancies." Abell does not believe that the public schools are the place to force her beliefs on anyone. But, she admits, "of course I hope that the students develop their spiritual side as well as their minds and bodies. That may do more to change their behavior than anything I could say to them."

THE COST TO CHILDREN AND TO SOCIETY OF IGNORING TEENAGE SEXUALITY

The cost to the children of the young men who live apart from the mother is enormous. Children living apart from their fathers are *five times* as likely to be poor and *twice* as likely to be high school dropouts. Seventy percent of the youngsters in long-term juvenile correctional institutions did not live with their fathers while growing up,[8] according to Louis Sullivan, who was Secretary of Health and Human Services in President George Bush's administration.

The two problems of absent fathers and of children growing up in poverty are often really one problem. As long as teenage mothers are left to take care of their children alone, many young women and their children will be dependent on government programs to get enough to eat and to keep a roof over their heads. Society will continue to have to pay billions in welfare costs and the children of these teenagers will be in danger of living their lives in poverty. Later in life, these children run a much higher risk of failing to complete high school and of getting in trouble with the law. These are "costs" to society that cannot be measured in the amount of welfare being paid out.

Even a part-time teenage father can make a tremendous difference to his child and the mother, according to Jeannette Abell, who has worked with middle- and high-school age parents in Ohio for ten years. She explains:

> *Even if he can't spend a lot of time with the mother, she feels better about herself that he still comes around and I think she's likely to be a better mother. And as the baby grows up, if it's a girl—but especially if it's a boy—it will have a sense of security from knowing who its father is. And it will understand better how its mother and father both have roles to play.*

THE DECISION TO STAY
OR TO "SPLIT"

Many who work with adolescent fathers report that the young men are often so demoralized by not being able to financially support their child that they drop out of the picture because of their feelings of shame or inadequacy.

"[Adolescent fathers'] understanding of a father's role is 'Where's the dollar?'" reports Priscilla Metoyer, director of the Young Parents Center of the Chicago Urban League. "And they don't have the dollar."[1]

Young men tend to connect the ability to take home a paycheck with their identity as men.

A 1974 survey found that among men in their late teens and early twenties, being a "good provider" was central to their masculinity. And among black middle-class fathers in a 1979 study, the answer to the questions "What do you think it means to be a man today?" and "What is the most important thing you can do for your children?" was the same: to be a financial provider.[2]

A study in Baltimore, Maryland, found that fathers who often saw their children were twice as likely to offer regular financial support to the family than those who hardly ever saw their children.[3] This is an excellent reason to encourage contact between father and child whatever the father's job situation when the baby is born, according to Chicago writer Steve Bogira. "[A] teen father may not be in a position initially to contribute money," Bogira writes, "but he's much more likely to [do so] when his situation improves if he's seeing his kids regularly."[4]

Bob Murdoch is setting up a young fathers' group in Lynn, Massachusetts, through Catholic Charities. He is a counselor who also works with the mentally handicapped. His program for young fathers is planned to go with one already in place for young mothers that provides transitional housing, health-care referrals, education programs, and counseling.

Murdoch admits it's not easy getting to the teenage fathers:

> *A lot of these guys think they have all the answers or at least act as though they do and sometimes it's hard to convince them they need help.*
>
> *But I think we have to get them at the "panic point." That's what I call the moment of confusion and stress when they first find out they're going to be fathers.*
>
> *Suddenly the girl's family is asking her, "Who is this guy, anyway?"*
>
> *Their own family is telling them: "I thought we told you to be careful! Do you know how much becoming a father is going to cost? What are you going to do about it?"*

> *And the guys are asking themselves, "Am
> I going to be able to handle it?"*
>
> *That's the moment when it's fight or flight
> time. If we can get to them and let them know
> there's help, they may be able to fight the panic
> and not run away. But the pressure's intense.
> And some of them just aren't going to be able to
> take it.*
>
> *Those are the ones who are likely to take
> off.*

When teenage boys find out they're going to be fathers, they wonder what this will mean for their future plans and for their relationship to the mother. How will her parents react? How will they tell their own parents? Who's going to decide if they should keep the baby, give it up for adoption, or end the pregnancy with an abortion?

Bryan Robinson, author of the 1988 book *Teenage Fathers*, quotes one adolescent father who describes his response on discovering that his girlfriend was expecting their baby:

> *I kinda got the feeling that it couldn't be
> true—I was just scared to death, didn't know
> what to do. Just a million things went through
> my mind. I was scared on the one hand having
> to consult my parents about the situation and
> then on the other hand I was kinda excited to
> know that I could be a father in nine months.[5]*

The teenage father suddenly has to go from being a carefree kid to becoming a fully responsible adult and many just aren't ready. They panic, and suddenly everyone—the mother, the couple's parents, friends, the world at large—becomes the enemy. They still think of themselves as adventurous and independent, like Indiana Jones, as one young father said, but people are trying to change them into a Pee-wee Herman.

Before, they could make decisions for themselves, but now they have to meet others' expectations.

So some teenage fathers flee.

WHEN YOUNG FATHERS
ARE SHUT OUT

Some teenagers who get a girl pregnant say they don't have a thing to say about what happens next. Take Cliff. He was just a few months away from high school graduation and had been going out with Janie for two years when they found out she was pregnant.

"There was nobody I could talk to," he remembers, "so I pretty much stayed by myself and worried. . . . I dreamed about how fine things were going to be—how we'd get married and about being a father. I knew it wouldn't be easy, but I could work at the mill and we could live on my family's farm. I just knew we'd make it."[6]

As it turned out, Cliff and Janie never got a chance to try to make it. Cliff's parents were pretty disappointed, but they said they would think about the couple's plans. But Janie's parents became furious. They refused to listen to what the teenagers wanted and told Janie that Cliff was a worthless creep.

They told Cliff to leave the house and when he tried going back two days later, Janie's father ordered him off the property and told him not to come back. Janie had been taken to a hospital for an abortion and was sent out of the state to finish high school.

Cliff and Janie never saw each other again.

"Both [Janie and I] had tried to be realistic and responsible," Cliff says. "But her parents took all of that away from us, and I was robbed of my right to have some say-so in what would happen to my child. I don't think I'll ever get over it."[7]

Teenage boys involved in pregnancies often are not included in the decision to abort a child or to put it up for adoption after it is born. The pregnant girl may not want to have a confrontation with the boy when they disagree about an emotional and difficult decision. Her parents may have advised her to keep the decision from him. Some expectant mothers who were in a casual relationship with the boy may not expect him to take an interest in her problem. Whatever decision is made, however, the teenage boy who is consulted is more likely to give the mother support, according to a 1985 study by Marcia Redmond of twenty-two teenagers who had been involved in teenage pregnancies.

Marcia Redmond, a family-planning coordinator working in the Waterloo area of Ontario, Canada, found that the teenage fathers who were employed were most likely to want to participate in the decision about the pregnancy. The young fathers who were included in discussions were usually willing to support the mother's choice even when they disagreed with it. They felt better about themselves because the mother and her physician or counselor thought their opinion was worth having.

Redmond concluded that most males involved in a

teenage pregnancy "wish to be included in this decision-making process and receive emotional and social support during this time. When not included, they feel confused and neglected."[8]

She warns that when the pregnant teen or those around her neglect the boyfriend, he may feel that he is the problem rather than part of the solution. The feelings of the young men may then "create problems for their girlfriends and professionals in obtaining a smooth resolution and outcome of the pregnancy."[9]

WHEN TEEN FATHERS
ARE PUSHED AWAY

"Society rewards the girl who gets pregnant—Aid to Dependent Children money, free health checkups—but nobody thinks about the father," says Juan Munoz, the founder and, for several years, the leader of ROCA's teen-fathers' program in Chelsea, Massachusetts, which helped out Stephen, Lisa, and little Stephen Anthony. "The mother gets all the attention," he continues, "and even if she's abusing the baby, the guy feels like he doesn't have any rights."

Jeannette Abell, who has worked for many years with young parents in Ohio, also agrees that young fathers often have good reason to feel shut out. "We set up the fathers to fail," she believes. "I've seen young dads get violent out of sheer frustration at not being able to get involved with their baby. We have to let them do as much as they can and let them know what *their* rights are." Abell points out that among the materials she is supposed to use in her young-parents' class is a brochure called "Males and the

36

Law" that is filled with terrifying threats about what will happen to a father, no matter how young in age, if he tries to hide income from support-enforcement agencies. "And they actually expect me to pass that out at my first contact with a fourteen or fifteen year old who's about to become a father!" she says in disbelief. "What kind of trust is that young man going to have that I'm here to help him after he reads that?" she wonders.

"A lot of young men say, 'I feel pushed away,' " says Fern Barushok, the director of Booth Memorial Hospital in Chicago. "But," she continues, "I think they push themselves away."[10]

Most of the girls Fern Barushok sees are in their early teens and most of them are not in serious relationships with the boys who made them pregnant. The boys "are not involved as fathers or boyfriends, or financial providers or anything," she remarks, "and they never will be."[11]

Fern Barushok is just speaking from her experience, of course. Many counselors feel that in keeping the girl together with her boyfriend, they are just setting the couple up to have more children. Many who work in this field don't want to encourage young teenagers to get into marriages that don't have much chance for success. And some teenage boys may be bad for the mother because of their history of violence, gang activity, drugs, and alcohol abuse.

But other counselors and social service people who work with young fathers believe that an attitude like Fern Barushok's that boyfriends of pregnant girls will *never* get involved may itself keep the boys away.

"A lot of the boyfriends of the pregnant girls we see don't see any role for themselves," says Suzanne Buglione. Ms. Buglione works with ACCESS, a service program in

Worcester, Massachusetts, for pregnant and parenting teens.

"It's almost as though their part has been taken over by the social-service agencies that are helping the girls," says Buglione. She points out that the professionals working with the mother sometimes scare the fathers away. When the pregnant girl's boyfriend comes forward, the first question may be, "What are you going to do about child support?" Financial support may be the only kind of support that the boyfriend is NOT able to provide, but he may just give up on staying involved if the emphasis seems to be on how inadequate he is as a provider.

Some programs insist that the father start making financial contributions to the baby immediately if he wants to spend time with his child. This is the so-called "No Pay, No Play" rule.

"We have to stop punishing the fathers who want to stay involved," adds Ms. Buglione. "An agency isn't a substitute for a parent. We can at least try to let the guys know what becoming a father is all about, teach them about the physiology of birth, let them tour the hospital where their baby's going to be born. If they're knowledgeable about what's happening, they're much more likely to participate."

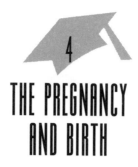

THE PREGNANCY
AND BIRTH

The French word "couvade" (pronounced coo-VODD) refers literally to "hatching eggs." In many Native American societies, particularly those in South America, an expectant father was expected to take on some of the characteristics of his pregnant wife. As the time for birth approached, the expectant father would not be allowed to go hunting or even to touch a sharp knife. It was taboo for him to lift anything that weighed too much. And as his wife went into the final labor, the father would himself retreat into seclusion. These "pregnant fathers" would often go through a sort of psychological "delivery" that seemed very real to them. Some even felt birth pangs.

THE COUVADE AND
SYMPATHY SYMPTOMS

Mainstream American culture may not seem to have that much in common with traditional Indian customs like the couvade. In fact, a significant percentage of expectant fathers in the United States report so-called sympathy symptoms.[1] The fathers-to-be suffer discomfort during the months that the mother-to-be of their baby is pregnant. Some of the symptoms they report are remarkably similar to pregnancy. Many expectant fathers gain weight or report nausea ("morning sickness"), loss of appetite, and even bloating of the stomach. One professional working with a group of fathers-to-be reported that they "gained an average of nearly fifteen pounds during pregnancy— just enough weight to support the birth of a healthy seven-pound baby."[2] And Karen Mott, a labor and delivery nurse at Beth Israel Hospital in Boston, Massachusetts, reports: "I've often heard fathers in the delivery room say 'I've gained every pound that [the mother] did during pregnancy.'"

The couvade and the sympathy symptoms seem to convey the deep-seated desire of many expectant fathers to take part in the birth of their child.

QUEASY, UNEASY, AND FEELING A LITTLE FAINT

No matter how much sympathy a teenager may feel for his pregnant wife or girlfriend, it can be a real trial of manhood for a teenager to watch her go through hours of difficult labor. Even young men who have led rough lives on the street may find themselves getting a little light-headed in the delivery room. Those who are intrigued by the process may still have mixed feelings. One nineteen-year-old who was present at his son's birth recalled, "Let's just say it was amazing—amazing and gross."

The delivery room may be an unnerving, even a horrifying, experience for some men. And the medical staff may not think the father should be there if there are complications or if the mother is under total anesthesia.

What's more, not even all expectant mothers feel comfortable having the father-to-be in the delivery room. Young mothers may find that it is awkward, undignified or immodest to have the father present. A father in his teens may take it as a criticism of him or as a denial of his importance during birth, especially if he's felt somewhat useless and left-out-of-the-picture during the pregnancy.

WHY LABOR AND DELIVERY ARE TOUGHER FOR TEEN PARENTS

The difficult circumstances of a teenage father-to-be may strongly influence how much he participates in the labor and delivery of his child. The chances are the pregnancy was unplanned and a young couple is likely to have greater financial worries as well as problems in their relationship.

Teens may also be even less comfortable than adults watching the pain, blood, and private parts of a young girl as she undergoes such vast—and messy—changes during childbirth. And teenagers often feel especially anxious about whether they will know how to take care of a newborn.

"In some instances, feelings of detachment and uselessness are brought into the delivery room by fathers who have come to feel unimportant during the pregnancy and don't feel comfortable or sure of themselves as caregivers," writes Jack Heinowitz, director of Parents As Partners, in San Diego, California, in his book *Pregnant Fathers*.[3]

Heinowitz stresses that fathers shouldn't blame themselves if they don't think they can handle the experience of a delivery room. It may be seen as a sign of weakness to "wimp out" on the mother and she may resent his squeamishness. But the upbringing or personality of some fathers may make it difficult or even impossible for them to be of help during the mother's labors.

One father was honest enough to confide to the authors of *The Father Book: Pregnancy and Beyond* that after thirty minutes in the labor room, he had had enough: "I know [my wife] thinks that my being there would be helpful to her, but I'd be so emotionally involved I'd probably screw things up. I don't feel I could be a comfort because I'd be too uncomfortable."[4]

SHARING IN THE WONDER

There is no direct connection between a father's participating at the birth of his baby and his later involvement in raising the child. But sharing the birth of a child often bonds parents together and can quickly bring a father very close to his baby at the beginning of its life.

One father who spoke with Jack Heinowitz for his book *Pregnant Fathers* about being in the delivery room with the mother talked about feeling "kind of an extrasensory communication going on" between the two of them. Another said:

> *It was like I was experiencing with her—*
> *almost in myself what she was going through.*
> *I couldn't feel the pain actually, but in my heart*
> *I was feeling for her. Sometimes I had to step*
> *back, to stay aloof from the intensity. . . .*

And a third father remembers that when the birth actually came, it was a kind of shock: "I was prepared for a beautiful, fantastic experience. I watched with disbelief as he popped forth all of a sudden. It took time for it to hit me—to realize that this was my baby, half me and half my wife."[5]

Participating in the birth of one's own child is a powerful, even mystical event for many fathers in and out of their teens.

ANDY, ADELA, AND THE BIRTH
OF AIDA MARIE

Andy is a young Latino father whose girlfriend, Adela, has just given birth to their daughter. It is Adela's second child, but Andy's first. The experience they shared when their daughter, Aida Marie, was born not only brought them together but also made Andy feel as though he'd really grown up. He's eager to point out, though, that he was no child even before his daughter was born.

"I hate that, when people talk about 'children having children,'" Andy says. He doesn't think of himself as a child. After all, he's an equal partner with Adela in raising two children. "I'm the father to Adela's son, Oscar," he explains, "even though it was by another guy. When my family talk about Oscar, they call him my 'man.'

"But we're even more of a team, my girlfriend and me, since Aida Marie was born. Adela was in labor nine hours. I could hardly stand it, seeing the pain she went through. But we were — we *are* partners."

Andy is a muscular twenty-one year old who has an impressive number of victories in amateur middle-weight boxing matches.

He isn't embarrassed talking about how it tore him up to see Adela going through her difficult labor and delivery. He talks about how hard it is to wear a macho mask all the time, as though a guy wasn't supposed to show any weakness, even when his girlfriend is going through a difficult labor.

According to Andy's girlfriend, Adela, Andy was a real comfort during her nine-hour labor ordeal. "I almost broke his hand, I was holding it so tight," she remembers.

But Adela almost makes it sound like an old *I Love Lucy* episode when she talks about how nervous Andy was as they were getting ready to go to the hospital, just before Aida Marie was born: "Andy was sweating. He didn't know what to expect and he was getting kind of hot and bothered. He was looking for the deodorant and he got so confused, I had to laugh when I saw him spraying his armpit with my hairspray.

"This was my second birth," Adela says, "so I knew what was going on in the hospital. Andy wanted to help, but he kept telling me what I should be doing. And he didn't really know!"

Adela wanted Andy by her side during the birth of Aida Marie, and he was doing everything he could to help. But she makes it clear that there was something a little funny about Andy trying to tell her how to get through her painful hours-long labor.

Adela's amused reaction to Andy's nervousness and uncertainty before and during her delivery make it clear that it's not always easy for men to find a comfortable role during the last stages of a woman's pregnancy. Perhaps Andy should have learned more about the process of delivery before he decided he could give her advice. But Adela is like many other young women when she expresses gratitude to Andy for being a hand to hold (in fact, almost break!) during her ordeal and Andy feels more of a man because he helped her through it.

AN EIGHTH-GRADE FATHER IN
THE DELIVERY ROOM

Ron was just fourteen years old when he and fifteen-year-old Donna went out to buy a home pregnancy test and discovered that Donna was pregnant—three months pregnant, as they later found out.

Living in a small city in the Midwest, Ron and Donna had been seeing each other for almost a year and wanted to have a baby together. Ron's parents were at first mad that Ron was "messing up" his life and suggested that Donna get an abortion. Ron was much more afraid that Donna would leave him than he was about messing up his life. After many discussions, Ron convinced his (and Donna's) parents that he would do whatever it took to care for the baby. It helped that his grandparents stood behind him and offered to assist financially.

As the pregnancy went on, the couple got more and more excited. At the urging of a teacher in his school, Ron went with Donna to six hours of training in the *Lamaze* method of childbirth. The Lamaze method prepares the mother and her "coaches" for a childbirth during which the mother is fully conscious, and the mother's labor pains are dealt with by relaxation, special breathing and pushing exercises, and lots of support and encouragement from the coaches.

"The Lamaze teacher showed me how I should help Donna breathe through her nose, in a rhythm," Ron remembers. "She had us practice where I would rub Donna's weak spots, wash her face with a cool rag, gently touch and rub her back—always rub down, never up, she said. The teacher also said I had to remember to tell Donna to relax, that everything was going fine, tell her she's doing a good job."

Through a class at school, Ron and Donna were also able to get a tour of the hospital in which she would have her delivery. The nurse who was guiding them showed them the different machines that might be used during the childbirth and how the delivery rooms were set up. By the time Donna's rhythmic contractions started, they felt prepared for what was to come.

Donna's mother and Ron were with the expectant mother in the delivery room in June 1994. "I felt awful for a while," Ron says. "I even started crying for all the pain I was putting her through. Then it started and I was helping, I was holding up her legs and doing all the stuff we'd learned in class." After two and a half hours of relaxation exercises, rhythmic breathing, and pushing (all to the encouraging words and comforting touch of Ron and her mother), Donna gave birth to a little girl. "She was so beautiful coming out," Ron remembers. He cut the umbilical cord of their new baby and they named her Sandra.

Sandra is three months old now and Ron is fifteen. The maturity and sense of participation he showed during Donna's pregnancy and the delivery have, if anything, increased. They are enrolled in a class at school for expectant and new mothers and their partners, where they have learned about the basics of caring for a newborn.

Sandra lives with Donna's family, but Ron sees them at least three times a week and he loves playing with the baby, feeding, and holding her. "I don't see Sandra every day," Ron admits, "but I pray for my baby every day. Even when I play football for the school, I'm playing for Donna and Sandra."

THE BENEFITS OF INCLUDING THE FATHER
IN PREGNANCY AND CHILDBIRTH

These days it's very common to see fathers-to-be accompanying their wives or girlfriends on visits to the doctor during pregnancy, to birth-preparation classes, and into the delivery room itself.

Going through the pregnancy and childbirth with the mother can also change the father's casual attitude to sex.

Danny is an eighteen-year-old, a member of three varsity sports teams, and, like Ron, attended Lamaze classes and coached his girlfriend through the delivery. As Danny puts it, "My girlfriend and I have cut down on intercourse since the baby. We don't want another kid now since my girlfriend's ready to graduate from cosmetology school and I want to go to college next year. We both understand what having a baby means and we never have sex except with both a condom and a spermicide cream."

Ron also believes that the experience of participating in Donna's pregnancy and the delivery of Sandra have changed their relationship for the better:

> *I want our relationship to last, so I try to get my mind off just having sex and we use protection now when we make love. When I went with her to the Lamaze classes, it helped convince her that sex wasn't all there was, all I was feeling. I still want her to know there's more than that and we go out together more now and do things together with the baby. And I try to be real supportive, like I was when Sandra was being born, try to feel what Donna's feeling and not put her down.*

Participation in the mother's pregnancy and the delivery may bring the couple closer, open the father's eyes to his importance in the welfare of his baby-to-be, and even make him more mature and responsible in the future when it comes to bringing children into the world.

The birth is also a good time (and is sometimes the last chance) for social-service workers or child-support enforcement agents to contact the father and try to involve him in the future of his child. A 1994 report from the Philadelphia-based Public/Private Ventures points out:

> *Hospitals are the most likely locations for inform- ing young and unwed fathers of their obliga- tions and rights under the law, and for starting the process of [determining fatherhood] early. . . . [M]any young fathers are present at the birth of their child or see them at the hospital soon after- ward—including some who have little or no commitment to the child's mother.*[6]

The report goes on to suggest that this may be the best time to intervene, when the young father is likely to be most eager to participate in raising his baby. The teenage father may never again be so open to acknowledging pater- nity (fatherhood) of his child, particularly if it links "early declarations of paternity with referrals to education and employment-directed services—instead of immediate financial obligations. . . ."[7]

5
ACKNOWLEDGING PATERNITY

When a baby is born to a married couple, the husband, who is assumed to be the father, has the same rights and obligations as the mother. Many teenage mothers and fathers, however, are not married when their child is born. Unmarried parents sometimes disagree over who will make the decisions about custody and visitation rights. A struggle also can occur between the couple and "the system"— the courts and social service agencies—over paternity issues.

Some questions that often arise are:

• Can the supposed father be sure that he *is* the father, since the mother may have had unprotected sex with other men?
• Can the mother get child support for her baby when a boyfriend, or former boyfriend, denies he is the father?
• Can an unwed father get visitation rights with his child if the mother doesn't get along with him anymore?

- Will young parents reveal the identity of the father to a public agency like welfare or social security when they think they have more to lose than to gain?

WHY TEENAGE PARENTS DON'T ESTABLISH PATERNITY

The recent scientific advances involving DNA, the genetic material carried in each cell of the body, make it possible to name the father of a child with almost 100 percent accuracy. Courts now routinely use this method to establish paternity, that is, legally identify the father. Yet teens rarely pursue these options when claims of paternity are disputed. Less than 3 percent of the fathers involved in court cases to establish paternity are eighteen years old or younger.[1]

Young unwed mothers do not try to establish the paternity of the child for several reasons. Some do not understand their legal options. Others realize that the father has abandoned them. The father may still be in school and unable to pay child support anyway. Some mothers are on welfare and are afraid that naming the father will reduce their benefits. Others may not want to get into a long-lasting association with the father of the child. Also, if a girl had sex under a certain age—sixteen years old in most states—she could expose her older boyfriend to prosecution for statutory (legally punishable) rape, even if the girl had consented to sex.

These reasons can keep a young father from acknowledging paternity as well. In addition, he may doubt he is the father or consider it the mother's responsibility to avoid getting pregnant. Some fathers have tried to persuade their partner to get an abortion or place the baby for adoption, and then walked away when she doesn't take their advice. Some prefer to keep their support and contributions "under the table," especially if the mother is on welfare, instead of formally stepping forward as the father. When the mother collects welfare, the amount of money she receives from the father is subtracted from the amount the welfare agency must pay her, with no advantage to the mother or the child.

Even though a court will not force a student to drop out of high school and get a full-time job to support his baby, it may require him to make a token payment (usually only five to ten dollars a week). Yet some teens do not want to work even part-time. And if a teen father is working, he may not want to sacrifice his own well-being for that of a woman he doesn't care about and a child he'd rather forget. He'd rather just keep his paternity quiet.

CONVINCING YOUNG FATHERS TO CLAIM PATERNITY

Betty Cook, who counsels young mothers and fathers in the Teen Advocate Program in Baton Rouge, Louisiana, expresses how hard it is to convince young parents to establish paternity. "We always try to get the father's name from the girls who come to see us," she says. Only 15–20 percent of the mostly African-American young unwed mothers in the program have boyfriends who want any part of fatherhood. One reason for the low percentage is that the girls who come to the program are struggling to cope with their pregnancy or new baby on their own.

When she sees the young women during appointments at the health clinic associated with the Teen

Advocate Program, Betty Cook does her best to convince the mothers to name the father and give their baby his name:

> *We try to tell the mothers that they have to think of what's best for their baby. Once the baby has a legal father, it can get inheritance rights from the father's family and the father gets the chance to see his baby even if the mother's family doesn't approve of him. Also, if anything happens to the father and he dies or gets killed, which happens around here sometimes, his baby may be able to get Social Security benefits.*
>
> *When the fathers are in the picture, we try to tell them that they have something to contribute to their baby's future, and not just money. There are things they can teach their baby that the mother can't. And we tell the boys, "If you don't think enough of the child to give it your name, you don't think anything of it."*

Betty Cook has no illusions that she can convince most of the young fathers she counsels to claim paternity, but she has had some success in convincing them to give their names to their children. Even this small step may be a big advantage for the newborn baby. The very act of sharing a name with a child may bond a father to a newborn. When a father gives a baby his last name, it is more likely that there will be a close relationship between him and his child. He will probably help more with the financial burden of raising the child, according to a 1980 study of teenage parents and their offspring.[2]

Some fathers who do not share their last name with

their son will give him their first name to emphasize their connection. One study in 1986 found that the sons of teen fathers were more likely to have the father's *first* name than his last name (68 percent versus 53 percent).[3] For some young fathers this may be a way of avoiding legal paternity while still passing on at least part of their name.

There are other reasons why it's in the child's best interests to have a legal father:

Medically, it is important to know of any hereditary diseases in the father's family that may be passed on to his child.

Psychologically, children want to know where they came from. It can be a serious blow to their self-esteem to find out later in life that their father refused to acknowledge them. A legal father has the right to visit his child on a regular basis and children usually have a healthier development in their childhood and adolescence when at least two people are interested in their welfare.

Financially, the establishment of paternity may mean that the child is eligible for health insurance through the father's medical-care plan and military benefits if the father is a member of the armed forces. The child may also gain inheritance rights. Once the father has acknowledged paternity, he is legally required, even if he is still a minor, to provide for any children of his until they are eighteen years old.

The children of teenage parents are likely to have little or no medical coverage, their psychological and emotional development will probably be more difficult, and they are likely to grow up in a financially disadvantaged household. It adds one more difficulty for these children when parents do not provide a legal father.

CHARLES BALLARD'S INSTITUTE FOR RESPONSIBLE FATHERHOOD AND FAMILY DEVELOPMENT

Charles Ballard, founder and president of the National Institute for Responsible Fatherhood and Family Development in Cleveland, Ohio, believes that a young father's first responsibility is to claim his child as his own and legally establish paternity. Ballard got his inspiration for the Institute in the 1970s while working in the maternity ward of a Cleveland hospital.

As Ballard told William Raspberry in a 1992 interview in *The Washington Post*:

I kept noticing all these mothers and babies, but no fathers. I started collecting the names of the fathers and visiting them after work, just to talk to them. Before I knew it, I had six different groups of these young fathers in various parts of Cleveland meeting and talking about everything from paternal responsibility to childhood development and reproductive health.[4]

In the years since the Institute first began working with young fathers in 1982, it has reached over two thousand young men, and more than half of these have gone to court to claim paternity of their children.[5] The process of making young men into young fathers, however, only starts with establishing legal paternity.

54

The ambitious set of programs at the Institute also reaches out to other family members. In "Family Resource Enrichment Experiences," two or three generations of a family learn together about childhood nutrition, goal-setting, and resolving arguments. There is also a program on conflict management for grandparents and one on positive male role models for male children of single mothers. Each of these efforts expands the network of people the father can call on to help him fulfill his responsibility towards his child.

Teen fathers who have received training in child care can get involved in a cooperative babysitting service. They can also join a four-month training program in sales and business leadership that instills self-confidence and prepares them for successful employment. And since most of the young men involved in the Institute are from predominantly black sections of Cleveland, some programs emphasize issues like leadership, empowerment, and ending drug abuse from the African-American perspective. One program is given in churches, schools, and community centers to junior high school students. It draws on black history and traditions to help young men make better life choices.

Ballard has discovered that when participants at the Institute work as volunteers with new members, the younger man finds a "brother figure" who can make up for the loss of the "father figure" and the older member gains self-esteem through his success in helping someone else. Some achieve the confidence they need to acknowledge the paternity of their babies, stick with their schooling or job, and cooperate with their child's mother to raise their children successfully.

The image of the fatherless babies and their overwhelmed young mothers in the hospital maternity ward in the 1970s has remained with Charles Ballard. As he told an interviewer on CBS's "This Morning" program just before Fathers' Day in 1992, "The best thing fathers can do for their children is to love their mothers."[6] The Institute has worked for over a decade to encourage and enable young fathers to do right by their child and the mother. Ballard and his colleagues have helped over a thousand young men choose to take on the responsibilities of fatherhood and improve their babies' lives as well as their own.

6
COPING WITH PARENTHOOD

Where does a teenage father turn if he decides that he is going to be involved in bringing up his child? Not surprisingly, the answer is that he usually tries to talk over the change in his life with the mother of his child, with his friends, and with his relatives.

STRATEGIES FOR COPING

One 1983 study of teenage fathers who were involved with their new babies found that all but six out of twenty teenage fathers reported that they coped with the stress of recent fatherhood by speaking with the people closest to them.[1] Those who were able to talk to their dads about the experience of fatherhood, for instance, drew comfort from sharing experiences with them.

Only four of the twenty young fathers looked at pamphlets about parenting given to them at the hospital where their child was born or read books about child care to prepare themselves for fatherhood. But seven of them tried to cope with becoming a father and trying to get ready for the future by reexamining their own past and appraising how good their own parents were in raising them. And fully 60 percent of the young fathers "fantasized about fatherhood and the baby and daydreamed of being in different situations with their children, outlining the kinds of things they would teach them."[2]

But the young fathers in this study did more. All twenty young men either got a job after being unemployed or quit school to get full-time work so they could help support their child. Six of the twenty reported that becoming a father "had made them settle down, and they had ended their partying, drinking, and fighting,"[3] spending more time with married friends and less with single young people. The authors of the 1983 study concluded:

> *To prepare for parenthood, all fathers [in the study] involved themselves in some new or additional activity to improve their financial situation. Most fathers helped to prepare for their baby by engaging in such activities as buying clothes or fixing up rooms. . . . Only a few fathers coped with upcoming parenthood by redirecting their life away from past social activities. Those who did viewed the change as a sign of "growing up."[4]*

Unfortunately, this sample does not reflect the harsh reality of teenage parenthood, since it includes only young men who are somewhat involved with their child. While many young fathers do "grow up" and take an active role in supporting their baby and its mother, a large number of teenage fathers will not even acknowledge they *are* the fathers and even fewer decide to marry their baby's mother.

In the past, social-service agencies that counseled teenagers about pregnancy and child care tried to convince them that they should marry and make their child "legitimate." More recently, many counselors have concluded that so-called shotgun marriages, where the father is pressured to marry the mother, may not be in the best interest of mother, father or child. Nevertheless, everyone agrees, a child is better off with a legal father.

WHEN IS MARRIAGE A GOOD IDEA?

The word "bastard" has an ugly sound to it. The idea of unmarried parents is distasteful or even sinful to many in our society (though less so in recent years), and some young parents marry just to keep their child from being "illegitimate," another word with a nasty sound.

But from a child's point of view, it may be more important to have its father around than to have him married to the mother. And if the child lives with its parents and other relatives—especially grandparents—the existence of a marriage certificate by itself may not be all that important.

Only about one-third of unmarried young men who fathered children as teenagers married the mother within a year of the birth, according to a study published in 1987 by William Marsiglio, a sociologist at Oberlin College. But about half of all teenage fathers lived with their baby just after its birth.[5]

In fact, there are some indications that early marriage may actually interfere with the young father's ability to complete his education and find work that will support his new family. According to William Marsiglio's 1987 paper: "Teenage fathers whose first child was [conceived during marriage] have the poorest high school completion patterns [of any teenage fathers], even worse than the patterns observed among those responsible for an unplanned birth at a relatively young age."[6] One explanation is that more married than unmarried fathers feel it's their responsibility to quit school in order to provide for their child. These fathers may be shortsighted: the less education they receive, the less likely they are to get a job with a good salary and a good future.

More than one million teenagers in the United States are married (about one in every ten men and women between fifteen and nineteen), but fewer than four out of ten teenage marriages last more than five years[7] and marriages entered into by parents under eighteen years old are almost three times as likely to break up as marriages in which the first child was born after the parents were twenty-two years old.[8] But in the marriages that do last, there is more contact between father and child and a better relationship between the parents than for unmarried couples, according to a five-year study of young mothers in Baltimore, Maryland, published in 1976.[9]

The pressures on young couples with or without a baby who decide to marry can be overwhelming. They are probably both still "finding themselves" and changing from year to year, sometimes even from month to month. The chances are they do not have much money and feel isolated if most of their friends are still single. Often, they differ on the amount of commitment each brings to the relationship and each other.

The arrival of a baby can place added stresses on the relationship between the mother and father. The existence of a marriage certificate is not going to keep them from having problems. Sometimes the child can seem like a burden that just won't go away. One nineteen-year-old father complained: "My wife and I just don't get enough time together anymore. We can't do some of the things we'd like to do like just run out and see a movie. . . . If we get in bed and try to talk, the baby will be crying in the next five minutes. They're just always there and you can't run from them."[10]

Differences in outlook and priorities may not become apparent until the pressures of pregnancy and child care start to take their toll. A sixteen-year-old mother married to a young father described what changes he made once she got pregnant—and what changes he *didn't* make:

> *When I first moved in [with the father], I was pregnant and he was going out with his friends. Or he would party in the front yard with them, and this was every night. . . .*
>
> *When I was about seven months pregnant, I told him, "Look, the baby is going to come. We have to make some changes." He finally realized what I was talking about. . . . His friends stopped coming for a while.*
>
> *But then they started coming back when I had the baby. I was in bed with the baby and they were outside partying. I told him we had to change because of the baby. I was tired. As time went on, he started making some time for us.[11]*

But the changes didn't last and about a year later, the couple separated and the mother moved back with the baby to her family.

Other couples find it hard to get to know each other and work on problems that come up in their marriage because they are so busy with the new baby. The father of one bride noticed that the couple never had time to get to know each other. "The emotional turmoil of an unwanted pregnancy for a teenager in high school, the emotion within the family—all these things take away from the focus of the marriage," the grandfather concluded.[12] He had tried in vain to talk the couple out of getting married six weeks after the baby was born, and the marriage only lasted three months.

Sometimes, the pressure to get married comes from the father's or mother's parents once they find out about the pregnancy. But Jeanne Warren Lindsay, the author of several books on teenagers, pregnancy, and marriage, warns that grandparents-to-be should be careful about forcing a marriage on a young couple just because a baby is expected. She writes: "Generally, the marriage decision should be made as separately from the pregnancy as possible. Many pregnant teens have wisely told me, 'Getting married because I'm pregnant wouldn't work. Two wrongs don't make a right.' This can be a difficult concept for parents who feel strongly that marriage is a necessary part of having children."[13]

In general, though, the participation of grandparents can be a lifesaver to a young couple trying to start a new life with their baby. Many teenage parents without means of their own find that their parents and in-laws are ready to provide them with financial support, a place to live (at least temporarily), and advice and help with child care while the teenagers finish their education or try to land their first jobs.

YOUNG PARENTS AND THREE-GENERATION LIVING

Among the approximately 50 percent of teenage fathers who live with their child shortly after its birth, one-fifth are in a household with at least one of their child's grandparents.[14] So, about one in ten adolescent fathers lives with one or more of his baby's grandparents, usually in his girlfriend's or wife's family. Far more adolescent mothers live with a parent shortly after their baby's birth, as many as eight in ten, according to a study of three hundred low-income teen mothers in Baltimore, Maryland.[15]

For a young mother, the help she gets from her family can make a tremendous difference. The young women who live with their families are "most likely to rely on their parents for child-care advice, and psychological support and to receive help with child care and in returning to school. . . . [They] were more likely to have graduated from high school, to be employed , and not to be on welfare. Mothers living with spouses were least likely to receive money or nonfinancial contributions from parents or relatives."[16]

For the young father, the involvement of his girlfriend's or wife's family can be a mixed blessing. On the one hand, the mother is receiving help with money, child care, advice, and housing. On the other hand, he may feel shut out of involvement with his baby since grandparents are less likely to help if the father is living with the mother.

And the mother's parents may not have the same faith in the father's trustworthiness that their daughter does. One teen mom's parents tried to keep their daughter from seeing her nineteen-year-old boyfriend, Darin, after she had a child named Kelli because he didn't seem like a responsible person and he had been in trouble with the law, mostly for speeding tickets. The teen mother recalls:

> *My parents were strongly against having Kelli spend the night at her father's house. They didn't think she should even go over there without me because my mother thought they wouldn't take good care of her. But I told them this was the only way her father could accept the fact that he has a daughter, and he has to do that if he's going to be responsible for Kelli. . . .*
>
> *Darin did quite well with Kelli. I knew he would—I have a lot of faith in him, but my parents don't, and that's where we disagree.*[17]

There are also pluses and minuses when a young father moves in with his girlfriend's family, even when her family likes and accepts him. Patrick, a nineteen-year old father of a one-year-old son spoke of his experiences with Karen Gravelle and Leslie Peterson, the authors of *Teenage Fathers*, a 1992 collection of interviews with young dads. Although Patrick and his girlfriend Sharon were not married, her parents and three sisters welcomed the young couple into their home after Sharon became pregnant. Patrick felt a little trapped sometimes, but he admits that living together did bring them closer.

Patrick shared in taking care of their son after he was born and things seemed to be going fine. He got a promotion at work and decided to get a college degree. But in time, he found it more and more of a burden to be living in Sharon's home: "I needed space. It's kind of crowded over there. I wasn't used to living in a house with five women. I needed privacy just for myself."[18]

Patrick moved out of Sharon's home about a year after their son was born, but he still sees his child every day and expects to marry Sharon in time. It is to her family's credit that they have supported the young parents and trusted them to make their own decisions about marriage and living arrangements. Patrick and Sharon have both shown a lot of maturity in the choices they have made. Her family has been able to help them without forcing the couple into an early marriage or insisting that Patrick not move out. Clearly, their baby is the winner in all of this.

WILLIE'S STORY: THE STORY OF A SINGLE FATHER

It has become less unusual in recent years for a single father to be the primary person caring for his child, usually because the mother has decided to leave him with the sole responsibility for the baby. Willie is one such single parent who has been able to raise his son with only the help of his family and a lot of determination.

Willie was nineteen when Deondrae (pronounced dee-ON-dray) was born. The mother, who isn't really in the picture anymore, was eighteen. Willie has noticed that people always ask him the same question. "When people find out I'm raising my son without the mother, they want to know, 'Was your son planned?'" Willie says. "Well, I guess you can't say Deondrae was planned," he continues, "but I was there when he came out and I can tell you, when you see your baby's head popping out, hey, you got your plan right there."

Willie's biggest fear when he found out his girlfriend of three years was pregnant was that they might not stay together. He hated to think she might drag his child over to some new family.

"I couldn't stand that," says Willie, "if there was some guy there who'd be hittin' my kid on the head sayin', 'Hi! I'm Daddy!'"

Willie was there at the hospital when Deondrae's mother started getting contractions. She was given pain medication and wheeled into a room, with Willie in hospital gown and mask right behind the doctor.

"I was just making sure she was all right and then, WHOOSH!, Deondrae came out like a bullet. That's what the doctor said I should call him, Bullet. I knew he was kidding, but anyway I had it all planned out. I knew I wanted to call my son Deondrae."

Now, father and son live with Willie's mother and some younger brothers and sisters of his, and Willie goes to school at a mostly black community college, majoring in business administration.

Willie didn't have to fight for custody of Deondrae. His baby's mother was told by the parents she lived with not to bother coming home if she brought the baby with her. Even when the girl was pregnant, she still liked going out to party and she was glad to let Willie and his family take care of the child once he was born.

It doesn't sound like Willie thinks there's anything so strange about a father raising a child without the mother. "Anybody can learn to take care of their kid," he says. "You know how to take care of yourself, you can take care of your child. I used to have questions, sure, but now people ask ME questions!"

Like Andy, the amateur boxer, Willie doesn't think people should talk about young parents as "children having children."

Willie's no child, even though he was only nineteen when his son was born and he has gotten a lot of help from his mother raising Deondrae, now three years old. He knows he's a better parent than his son's mother is ever likely to be. He intends to run his own business some day.

"Whatever I do, my son is always part of the picture," Willie insists. Deondrae may not have been the product of a planned pregnancy, but Willie's story makes it clear that fathers can be remarkably able at "mothering" and "fathering."

JOHN LASS AND "EVENING BREEZE"

The young fathers who attend the weekly "Evening Breeze" meetings with John Lass and other staff members from the Insights Teen Parent Program in Portland, Oregon, don't just talk about how to become good parents to their babies: they act it out.

John Lass, who is in his early forties and the father of two children himself, has been counseling teen fathers for over ten years. As he told a reporter from *Life* magazine in 1984, "A lot of these [young fathers] do not know what a father is supposed to do. Many of them had no fathers around. . . . But they can be just as nurturing as the mothers"[19] if they get a chance to learn. Through trial and error, he has come to believe that young men can be taught the skills they need to stay involved with their children not merely through discussions, but also through role-playing and group activities involving young children.

A typical meeting of the dozen or so members of "Evening Breeze" (about fifteen young parents, including some couples and four or five young men) might start with some warm-up movements to loosen up the group and then continue with a role-playing exercise to remind the parents what it was like to be a toddler. One person stands on a chair and another gets beside the chair on his knees. The "adult" on the chair then pulls on the "toddler's" hand and tries to walk him around the chair. The person playing the toddler gets a sense of what it's like to be pulled around when you're uncertain on your feet to begin with. The person on the chair realizes that to a young child an adult appears like an all-powerful giant with very strong arms.

"Evening Breeze" meetings last about two and a half hours (including pizza or a buffet-dinner break) and the four-person staff has created other exercises that teach the young parents how to:

• become comfortable with everyday activities like feeding, changing, and playing with a young child,

• help their baby acquire language skills and deal with issues like trust and separation as their child gets older,

• work out parenting responsibilities when the father and mother are themselves having problems in their relationship, and

• maintain self-esteem and stay involved with their children even when things are going badly for them economically, academically, or emotionally.

Graduates of the "Evening Breeze" series receive gifts at the end of the series, including books about parenting and health problems, and also children's books (with tough, baby-proof bindings) to share with their kids.

"Evening Breeze" is only one of the services John Lass offers to young fathers in Portland. As Fatherhood Project Coordinator and Counseling Supervisor, he is involved in recruiting young fathers into programs, helping them with school, employment, and family problems, and educating them about family planning and sexually transmitted diseases. But the "Evening Breeze" meetings show that young fathers who get restless sitting still and listening to lectures may learn more about their babies and themselves through activities that involve their bodies as well as their minds.

YOUNG FATHERS OF COLOR

"When I'm on the street with my little son Terence, Jr., people stop me— even people I don't know, black and white—to ask how he's doing. I can tell they're thinking, 'Am I seeing things or what?'

"It's great that they see a young black man like me taking care of my child, but it gets me down that they're so surprised."

—Terence, twenty years old,
Roxbury, Massachusetts

THE BAD RAP ON BLACK TEENAGE FATHERS

The overwhelming majority of teenage fathers are not African-Americans. Yet in the public mind, it is African-American men who have been most closely connected with the stereotype of someone irresponsibly getting a woman pregnant and then leaving her with the child. According to this stereotype, the child then grows up without any personal commitment or financial support from him.

This easy conclusion contains one important flaw. In general, blacks in American culture have always been poorer than whites, from the time they were brought here as slaves up to the present day. A teenager who is unable to contribute financially to the welfare of his son or daughter may feel he has nothing else to give. Moreover, the mother of his child (or her family) may share this opinion and exclude him from involvement.

The differences between ethnic groups become much smaller when *disadvantaged* whites are compared with other groups.

A 1984 study found that while black or Latino teenagers were much more likely to become fathers than all teenagers put together (15 percent for blacks, 11 percent for Latinos, and 7 percent for all teenagers), the rate of teenage fatherhood for disadvantaged whites was 12 percent, much closer to the number for all blacks and all Latinos. On the other hand, only 5 percent of white teenagers who were *not* disadvantaged became fathers.[1]

It seems fair to conclude that teenagers who share economic hardship are more likely to become fathers early in their life, whatever ethnic group they're part of.

How do black teenage dads behave once they've fathered a child?

Again, a simplistic view is misleading. Young black fathers are less likely to live with their child than Hispanic or whites, even poor whites. Nearly 60 percent of economically disadvantaged whites and almost 80 percent of higher-income whites lived with their babies, according to a 1987 study of over five thousand teenagers. By comparison, just under half of the young Hispanic fathers and only 15 percent of the black teenagers shared a household with their child.[2]

But living with one's child is not the only standard for how involved a young father is with his baby. A 1986 study of one hundred African-American teenage fathers found that eighteen months after the birth of the baby, about 12 percent lived with their child, which is very close to the 15 percent of black teenagers found in the study of five thousand teens from 1987. But 25 percent saw their baby on a daily basis. A further 28 percent had contact between three and six times a week. Adding those numbers together, we find that two-thirds of the black teenage fathers studied saw their child at least every other day. Only 2 percent reported that they had no contact with their child at all.[3]

SPECIAL PROBLEMS AND PROGRAMS FOR THE YOUNG BLACK FATHER

Even though research like this 1986 study has found that young black fathers are often involved in their children's lives, there is still a gap between them and other ethnic groups that needs to be explained. Linda Anderson Smith, a researcher and teacher at North Carolina State University, says African-Americans face three particular obstacles to full participation as parents:

1. Black Americans historically have had fewer economic opportunities, and the rate of unemployment for

African-American men is the highest of any group. Without the means to support a family, many walk away from responsibilities like fatherhood.

2. Young black men often believe that whatever effort they put forward will be frustrated by a society that does not respect them; eventually, they simply stop trying to make it in a hostile environment.

3. The future seems to many of these young men to hold very limited possibilities and so they put all their energy into getting through the present moment. To quote the black writer Langston Hughes's poem, their hope for success and happiness becomes "a dream deferred" (put off) and eventually the dream dies.[4]

Even when a young black man decides to fight the odds and be a real father to his child, he may encounter ridicule and even open hostility from those around him. William Allen, a graduate student at the University of Minnesota who wrote his master's thesis on young black fathers, reports after interviews with many adolescents that:

> *Among their friends—sometimes from their own brothers or other family members—these men get the message that they're "suckers" to try to get an education or to keep up ties with their girlfriend after she gets pregnant. They come to believe that people in their community can't rely on society as a whole to help them out. It's like black men and women have to use each other, that what the woman gets, the man loses. They want to be involved with their baby, but when some problem comes up between them and*

the mother, the message they get from those
around them is: "You're a fool to stick around.
There's lots of other fish in the sea."

Dr. Melvin Moore, clinical director of the Youth and Family Center, a nonprofit agency near Los Angeles, believes that outreach programs to young minority fathers can make all the difference to teenagers who are struggling with the consequences of becoming fathers and not finding much encouragement or assistance from society, family, or friends. Dr. Moore, whose degree from Harvard is in clinical psychology, believes that "society doesn't come up with money for teen fathers unless they're in trouble and break the law. We have sixteen-year-olds teaching the twelve-year-olds what it is to be men!"

At the Youth and Family Center, they have been working since the mid-1980s to find solutions that have less to do with the race of the young father and more with trying to change the "man within." Dr. Moore has reservations about putting too much stress on the race of the young fathers rather than trying to build self-esteem:

> *An Afrocentric approach to the problems*
> *these young men face might be one thing you*
> *could do, use a historic approach and then build*
> *on it to instill black pride. But sometimes I've*
> *heard young fathers make excuses for themselves*
> *based on their [African-American] ancestry and*
> *all that entails, when they've never really had a*
> *direct experience of racism and don't even min-*
> *gle with Anglos. They figure they're victims, so*
> *they don't put their best foot forward.*
>
> *I think it's more important to teach them*

that self-esteem comes from achievement, from the relationships you have and the way you treat people. We try to show them how important they are to their kids and our program stresses achievement as the way to build up their self-esteem and *to give them the tools so they can take the responsibility to be real fathers.*

In recent years, some Afro-American filmmakers and rap artists have tried to present the reality of teen fatherhood in the black community. Like Dr. Moore, they don't try to ignore the racial part of the problem, but the stories they tell stress the themes of personal responsibility and achievement that he believes are so important to young black fathers.

A MOVIE AND A RAP ABOUT TEEN DADS

In general, popular culture does little to shatter the myths about young fathers and or to change people's idea of black teenage fathers as uncaring, irresponsible people who get a girl pregnant and then walk away. In fact, television, movies, and popular music rarely portray young people of color except in stories that emphasize violent conflict or romantic situations that never seem to end in pregnancy and parenthood.

To help change these stereotypes, a talented young black filmmaker, John Singleton, and the rap group Ed O.G & Da Bulldogs have portrayed teenagers who are dealing with issues of individual responsibility and social pressure, and trying to come to terms with what it means to be a young father in the black community. In their works, these African-American artists have given a sense of hope and uplift to the young men in their community who are becoming parents for the first time.

JOHN SINGLETON'S
BOYZ N THE HOOD

John Singleton was only twenty-three years old when his film *Boyz N the Hood* came out in 1991. The movie takes place in a black neighborhood in gang-ridden South-Central Los Angeles. *Boyz N the Hood* depicts a divorced father and a former army man, Furious Styles, who takes up the parenting of his seventeen-year-old son Tre after Tre's mother decides that she wants to return to school. Furious has a calm exterior, but when he lectures Tre on avoiding gangs, we see the anger and bitterness he keeps inside. Furious may be stern with Tre, but he realizes that it will take strong talk to counteract the violent reality of the street.

When Furious learns that Tre has started having sex with his girlfriend, he asks his son: "You been using the rubbers I gave you, haven't you?" This sense of responsibility rubs off on Tre. He saves a baby, left unattended by its young mother, from being run over and lectures the mother: "Keep your baby out of the street. And change her diaper."

Singleton seems to be making the point that if Tre were without the strong guidance of his father, he would never have a chance to survive the mean streets of his "hood" (neighborhood). At the end of the movie Tre goes on to attend college. By taking on the responsibilities of fatherhood, even after years of absence, Furious has given his son a chance for security, self-esteem, and success.

In turn, when the time comes, Tre will have the inner strength and self-knowledge to raise his own children with both love and discipline. To use the language of Dr. Melvin Moore quoted earlier in this chapter, Furious has given Tre the "tools" he needs to resist the violence of the street and become a real man and, in time, a real father.

ED O.G & DA BULLDOGS' "BE A FATHER TO YOUR CHILD"

Rap music is about the last place you'd expect to find a plea for young fathers to accept their obligations toward their children. Some rap groups do focus on political or racial issues. But many if not most lyrics in rap music by male artists focus on the macho stereotypes of casual sex, indifference to responsibility, and, often, contempt for women.

Ed O.G and his "crew" grew up in the mostly black Roxbury neighborhood in Boston and recorded *Life of a Kid in the Ghetto* in 1991. They combine a playful fascination about sex with a healthy concern for its consequences. In one rap Ed O.G wants to have sex with a girl "until she screams and squirms," but he also says not to "sweat that/I got a jimmy hat [condom] for safety."

One track on the album, "Be a Father to Your Child," reflects Ed O.G's own experience growing up in Roxbury. He told an interviewer:

> *A lot of girls I know around my neighborhood have babies, and none of them are with the fathers. When I ask them "What's up?", they just say they can't stand the fathers or the fathers ain't doin' what they supposed to be doin'. . . .*

78

It's not like the old days anymore when you had
to marry a girl if you got her pregnant.[5]

The rap "Be a Father to Your Child" preaches the message of its title. Ed O.G raps, "Half of the fathers with sons and daughters don't even wanna take 'em/But it's so easy for them to make 'em." He criticizes the fathers who think just buying their child a lot of gifts is the answer: "It's not the presents, it's your presence and the essence/Of being there and showing the baby that you care."[6] He even puts down the young fathers who harass their child's mother when she takes up with another man and argues that if the new boyfriend is a good father to the child, the natural father should let him do the job.

Like John Singleton, Ed O. G stresses the importance of individual choice amid difficult social pressures. The popularity of these artists' work may be an indication that the message is getting through.

YOUNG LATINO FATHERS

Traditionally, in Hispanic cultures the father is "jefe de la casa" (head of the household) and, at least theoretically, what he says goes. Among Mexican-Americans, for instance, the father may be affectionate with his children, especially when they are small, "but his authoritarian [boss's] role is clearly established by the time children enter puberty. Whereas the mother is loved and adored, the father is feared and obeyed."[7] Household tasks like feeding the baby, keeping the house clean, or doing the dishes are purely women's work.

Even though these "macho" ideas are widespread in

Hispanic-American communities, younger Latinos tend to share them less and less. Research shows that there always was a large gap between what Hispanics accepted as the norms for women and men and what the reality actually was. A study as early as 1946 found that the mother in Mexican-American families may not seem to have much power in the family, but "she may actually dominate in all matters that affect her children. Hers may be the deciding voice in every important decision."[8] One young Latino showed skepticism about the difference in power his mother and father actually had in the household where he grew up: "My father did the talking . . . but it was my mother who really decided things."[9] Like others his age, this young man realized that, even for his father's generation, being the "jefe de la casa" didn't always mean having one's way.

According to traditional attitudes, the more children a Latino man has, the more manly he seems. If an unmarried girl gets pregnant, her father's honor is seriously damaged and she is often forced out of her parents' home, according to Mercer L. Sullivan, a researcher at Vera Institute of Justice in New York City. But when a pregnancy occurs out of wedlock, a young father's family "receives confirmation of his virility [masculinity] and is not disgraced in this way."[10] The young father who acknowledges paternity, however, is often under strong pressure to marry the mother and set up another household with her and the baby.

Interviews with young Latino fathers indicate that they view their sons differently from their daughters. One nineteen-year-old born in Guatemala, who had fathered two children, reported that he wouldn't mind bathing a baby boy or changing a son's diaper, but that he wouldn't feel comfortable handling his naked daughter because "people might get the idea I was doing something wrong with her. A man shouldn't be touching a girl like that."

Among many younger Latinos, the ultra-masculine ideal seems to be falling out of favor. Fathering many children to prove one's manhood and then only getting involved with one's children as the parent who disciplines them is no longer the ideal for many young fathers. "I hate to see guys coming along making babies while they're still kids," says Luis, a young father born in Puerto Rico now in his early twenties. "I was afraid to even hold my son Joshua when he was first born. Someone had to show me how. But when my girlfriend couldn't handle taking care of our son and moved back out of state, I learned how. Now Joshua lives with my family and his godmothers and godfathers take care of him while I'm at work. I'm lucky, but young kids, they should think about it before they have a baby."

REACHING OUT TO YOUNG FATHERS

It's just common sense that if you want to protect the future of a baby born to teenagers, you have to help the teenagers be good parents.

A few teenage fathers have primary responsibility for their child; some are equal partners in parenting. Nevertheless, many teenage mothers cope alone with parenting. So it's not hard to understand why programs concentrate their limited resources on the mother instead of the father.

Young women who have gotten pregnant and don't get the help they need from their partner, friends, or relatives usually seek out programs that help them with prenatal care, housing, education, and job training. Most teenage boys involved in a pregnancy, on the other hand, often need a lot of convincing before they will seek out help for themselves. Only *two* of ninety-five adolescent fathers would look to a social service agency if they needed help, according to a study of ninety-five teenage dads from 1981, and even fewer would try talking out their problems with a minister or teacher.[1]

When a group has set up a program with young fathers in mind, it often has a difficult job just getting them in the door. Many teenagers assume, often quite rightly, that any program staff member they meet is only trying to "help" them in order to get child-support payments out of them. "Often the young men are suspicious," explains Bryan E. Robinson, author of *Teenage Fathers*. They are not likely to get involved in a program, Robinson explains, "unless they are convinced that programs have something to offer beyond forcing them to assume financial responsibility for their children. . . . Young men are hesitant to take advantage of programs unless special efforts are made to reach them."[2]

These "special efforts" at reaching teenage fathers may include a lot of footwork. "We have to beat the bushes," says Ron Johnson, a former gang member and for many years director of a Teen Fathers program in Lawndale, near Los Angeles. He explains: "We speak at high schools, go to every coach in every school, to the churches and the streets. We go to hangouts where they sell drugs to get money for the child and girlfriend."[3] Athletes Coaching Teens, a program in Richmond, Virginia, used the popularity of professional athletes to reach players on high school sports teams with a message about pregnancy prevention and sexual responsibility.

Some try involving young fathers by inviting them to prenatal examinations of the mother and letting them hear the heartbeat of the baby in the womb. Others emphasize the importance of having male counselors in programs that target teenage fathers. "It is possible that agencies which are closely identified with providing services to young women may see a reluctance on the part of males to [use] their services,"[4] according to a 1987 study on young unwed fathers. The authors of the study point out that the agencies that work with teenage parents often center their services around the female. The almost all-female staffs will often direct "all services for males around the needs of female clients without awareness of the service needs of males."[5]

The problem, however, is not just one of programs that favor the mother. Many young fathers are simply afraid of becoming a father. Typical is the attitude of Maurice, a nineteen-year-old father involved with the Teen Father Collaboration (TFC), an ambitious network of programs that was set up in eight cities around the country for two years in the mid-1980s. Maurice remembers going to his high school counselor after he found out his girlfriend was pregnant. When the counselor told him about the TFC program, he recalls:

> *I just freaked out. . . . The child—I hadn't fully accepted the idea. I personally really didn't want to think about the matter. But the more my counselor spoke to me, the more I began to accept the idea. "What have I got to lose?" I thought. I realized I was just scared.*[6]

The special efforts that must be made to reach young fathers and to keep them involved in programs take a lot of time and energy, and many projects don't have the resources to do the job. A father who does get involved may not be as reliable as the counselors would hope, so the counselors have to show enormous patience. Even when staff members have set up job interviews or counseling sessions for young fathers, for instance, many fail to show up, according to a paper about the Teen Father Collaboration. According to this report, many of the young men involved in TFC programs "seemed to drop out of service programs, only to reappear after weeks or months had passed. As one counselor stated, 'these young men have not [developed] adult attitudes yet.'"[7]

It can be frustrating to work with teenagers who often don't respond to a helping hand when it is extended. Few groups in our society need help more (and get it less often) than teenagers living in urban poverty. And those teens who are also fathers have special problems that demand enormous patience from the counselors.

Not many programs that target teenage fathers last longer than a few years. Often projects are scheduled to get funding for only a couple of years and when the money dries up, the program dies. Programs sometimes start with too little funding or inadequate planning and never get off the ground. Staff members may feel overworked, underpaid, and unappreciated and they "burn out."

To find out what the status of programs for teen fathers around the nation is, more than forty programs for young fathers in fifteen states were contacted. Some are modest but long-lived programs, like the INSIGHTS Fatherhood Project in Portland, Oregon, which has emphasized one-on-one contact between a young father and his counselor for almost ten years. Others were well funded, like the demonstration and research project started in 1990 and coordinated by Public/Private Ventures in Philadelphia. This program, which published its initial progress report in fall 1992, has already set up projects for young unwed fathers in cities in six states: California, Florida, Maryland, Ohio, Pennsylvania, and Wisconsin.

Unfortunately, the message heard in talking with counselors and coordinators of many programs was that their resources had actually *decreased* over the past decade. Many programs follow the pattern of the Fatherhood Project in New York City, once run by the Bank Street College of Education and now administered by the Families and Work Institute. Many ambitious projects such as the Fatherhood Project that were set up in the mid-1980s had to be cut back when funding ran out.

(A listing of organizations with programs for teenage fathers or with resource materials available about starting and running such programs can be found in "Where to Go for Further Information," p. 109.)

A MODEL PROGRAM: OUR PLACE
IN EVANSTON, ILLINOIS

Considering how difficult it is to keep projects for young fathers going, a program such as Our Place, in Evanston, Illinois, which has lasted for almost fifteen years, must be doing a lot right. Evanston is not a big city (its population is about 70,000) but it has one of the oldest and most respected programs for teenage parents in the country. Since the project began in 1980, it has included special efforts to get teenage fathers involved with their children.

In Evanston, an ethnically diverse city near Chicago, about 20 percent of the population lives below the poverty line. The Our Place program gained wide attention when Daniel B. Frank wrote a book about his experiences as a counselor there, *Deep Blue Funk & Other Stories: Portraits of Teenage Parents* (1983).

Teenage fathers are recruited through their girlfriends or through young men already involved in Our Place activities, by outreach to high school and youth groups, and from referrals by juvenile court judges and probation officers. Our Place tries to get young fathers to attend support groups by sponsoring basketball games where the motto is: "If you want to play hoop, you have to do group."

Today, Our Place offers, among other programs:

- an infant development center called the "Teen Baby Nursery";
- teaching sessions on birth control, prenatal health, child care, and mother-father and parent-child relationships;
- vocational training, including an ambitious four-day-a-week nine-month program called "Teen Cuisine" which trains young parents—one-third of them young fathers—for jobs as chefs at restaurants and hotels;
- a young fathers' support group, led by a male counselor, where teenagers can share their problems and help each other in coming up with solutions.

Our Place has served as a model for projects around the country. Working within a relatively small community and starting with few resources, Our Place has grown and prospered for nearly fifteen years by showing ingenuity in recruiting young fathers and developing programs that actually work.

BRIDGING TWO PROGRAMS TO MAKE AN EVEN STRONGER ONE

Government policies often reflect a common attitude of officials and the general public that teenage fathers are a lost cause. Many who work with young fathers are frustrated by distant, uninformed bureaucrats who make policy for young fathers but who have never known any. Ed Woodley and Linnea Johnson-Scott, however, have reached out to help teenagers in Washington State by coming up with programs that address their needs. They have also brought the teenagers "close up and personal" with the officials who make decisions affecting the young fathers' everyday lives.

PROJECT MISTER IN SEATTLE, WASHINGTON

In the late 1980s, Seattle minority businessman Ed Woodley started a program—Project MISTER—aimed at reaching inner-city minority youth, specifically young fathers, in the Seattle area.

Project MISTER was designed to give young men the opportunity to change their lives. Many who have gone through the Project MISTER program had been involved in gang violence, some were themselves survivors of abuse or neglect as children, and all had wrestled with either the temptations or the consequences of alcohol and drug abuse. Project MISTER was designed to help a young man decide what goals to aim for, to develop attitudes that would help him reach the goals, and to make available to him concrete opportunities for education and employment. In general, Ed Woodley hoped to take the guys everyone else had given up on and make them into good parents and responsible citizens—a tall order!

Project MISTER included weekly group meetings, individual counseling about personal problems, and back-to-school and job-training programs. Woodley drew on resources of state agencies, local government, and community organizations. Even the Washington State Department of Wildlife got involved, sponsoring outdoor treks for young men in the program.

Ed Woodley had been able to use his connections with other minority businessmen in the Seattle area to set up a unique ceremony for the young fathers who complete the Project MISTER program. At the end of the year, a young dad who had met his personal goals was considered a "graduate." He was matched up with a mentor (an older and trusted adviser) from the local minority business community, who would remain involved with him after the ceremony was over. The mentor gave the young father a pair of hard-soled shoes and a new tie, both useful for job interviews. Just as important, the adult would take the time to show the teenager how to tie the tie. Then all the businesspeople and the young fathers would attend a formal dinner to celebrate the occasion. In 1992, 125 people were present at the Project MISTER banquet.

But exactly why were these people celebrating? After all, the young men had not gotten high school diplomas. Many were still out of work. Just owning a pair of new shoes or knowing how to tie a tie was not going to guarantee them a job.

People participate in a celebration because they think an important step in their lives is being taken that will change them forever and they want an event to remember it by. The young fathers in Project MISTER were celebrating that kind of change:

- First, they had become educated on issues like child care, domestic violence, substance abuse, and sexual responsibility in group and individual counseling sessions with Ed Woodley and others.
- Second, they had set and met positive goals for themselves—a first for many of the teenagers—and had started to change their behavior, whether as parents, as partners to their child's mother, or just as people with more than their share of problems.
- Finally, the young fathers had themselves gotten "fathers" that night and learning to tie a tie was only the first thing they could get advice on from their mentors in the months, or even years, ahead.

Many of the young men had never had a real father while growing up. The hard-soled shoes may have been the first thing of value they had ever gotten from an older male. Apart from the sessions with Ed Woodley, this may have been the first time a person with some success in life had taken an interest in their future. Now that they *had* "fathers," Woodley believed they were better able to *be* fathers.

Another way that Project MISTER tried to help the young men become better fathers of their children was to make sure that they didn't have more unwanted kids and, to do this, Woodley used a learning package called "Draw Your Conclusion." That's how he met Linnea Johnson-Scott, who was working to put the "Draw Your Conclusion" curriculum into effect in Washington State.

OFFICE OF SUPPORT ENFORCEMENT
IN OLYMPIA, WASHINGTON

Olympia, the capital of Washington State, is about an hour and a half drive by car from Seattle, where Project MIS-TER is based. Linnea Johnson-Scott worked for the State Office of Support Enforcement in Olympia. Her office had the job of collecting child-support payments from fathers who are often reluctant to pay. Agencies that try to collect child-support usually concentrate all their energy on pursuing fathers (and less often mothers) who fall behind in their payments. But Johnson-Scott worked to implement a statewide project based on the "Draw Your Conclusion" curriculum, a teenage pregnancy-prevention program developed by the Center for Support of Children in Washington, D.C.

Johnson-Scott had convinced the Office of Support Enforcement that the curriculum she was putting into practice would help prevent teenage pregnancies before child-support payments from the father ever became an issue. The program tried to make teenagers of both sexes aware of what an unplanned pregnancy can mean for both partners. It taught them to "draw your conclusion" about the possible results of having unprotected sex.

She and Ed Woodley had joined together to bring the "Draw Your Conclusion" message to the young fathers of

Project MISTER. Now they were combining forces to bring together ten of the fathers from Project MISTER and a group of government officials who made policies that affected young fathers. Up to this time, few of these officials had ever met a minority teenager, let alone an adolescent father, except as an unwilling client at a social-service agency, as a suspect in a crime, or as a defendant in a court of law.

BRIDGING THE TWO PROGRAMS

What would happen when the bureaucrats saw the black T-shirt that Terry, a seventeen-year-old member of Project MISTER, was wearing? In large white letters, the shirt read "SHUT UP BITCH!"

Linnea Johnson-Scott was riding in a mini-van in May 1992 with Ed Woodley, Terry and nine other young fathers from Seattle to the meeting in Olympia she and Woodley had spent months getting together. The government officials—mostly middle-aged white men and women—represented the local prosecutor's office, state policy-planning agencies, and federal departments in Washington, D.C. Johnson-Scott and Woodley hoped by bringing policymakers face-to-face with young minority fathers to change the bureaucrats' attitudes.

But what was going to happen when the suspicious bureaucrats in Olympia got a look at the sexist, vulgar, and threatening message on Terry's t-shirt? Would they decide that black teenage fathers were just as hopeless and unreachable a bunch as they'd always suspected?

"I was really impressed by how Ed handled it," recalls Johnson-Scott. She says:

*Ed didn't raise his voice, but he didn't beat
around the bush, either. He told Terry he could
either turn the t-shirt inside-out and put it on
backwards, where the words wouldn't be noticed,
or put on his sweatshirt and keep it on over his
shirt throughout the meeting. Ed never gave
Terry the choice of not participating.*

*An hour went by and we were almost in
Olympia when Terry finally put on the sweatshirt. We went to the meeting and, thank God,
he kept it on.*

The meeting itself was not without its share of fireworks.
Ed Woodley recalls that the language the young fathers
used in talking to the bureaucrats was not what the adults
were used to hearing. "When the guys ran out of words,
they used street language," he explains with a laugh, "but
they got their point across."

Whatever words they used to express themselves, the
teenagers knew more about child-support enforcement
and paternity law than the adults had expected. Terry
showed a flash of temper when he talked about the way
the authorities come after young teen fathers for child
support but don't penalize young mothers who "work the
system" by cheating the Welfare Department and using
the courts to shut out fathers who *do* want to be involved
with their child.

Ed Woodley himself got a little angry listening to a
state prosecutor say that teenagers didn't really think
much about it when the state came after them for child-
support payments. "It's only a small portion of their lives,"
the prosecutor maintained. Woodley recalls asking the

prosecutor, "You mean if you have a thirteen-year-old kid and the state's coming after him for money, that's not going to make any difference to him? What's that going to mean for him at eighteen, at twenty-three?"

The prosecutor who had something to learn about what it felt like to be a teenage father was listening hard that day. When the Project MISTER "graduation" ceremony took place the next month, in June 1992, the prosecutor was there, teaching Rick, a young father, how to tie a tie. A few months later, Johnson-Scott was delighted when Rick walked into her Office of Support Enforcement to announce that he had legally acknowledged paternity of his child and was ready to formally take on the responsibilities—and the rights—of fatherhood.

The message on Terry's t-shirt, offensive as it was, may have been not so much a threat, telling someone to shut-up-or-else. It may have been an expression of frustration from someone not used to being heard who was asking: "Someone, won't you listen?" Fortunately, people *were* listening that day and what the young fathers of Project MISTER had to say moved a hardened state prosecutor to try to make a difference in one young man's life.

LEARNING THE LESSONS OF MODEL PROGRAMS

Our Place in Evanston, Illinois, is now part of a network of programs around the state called Family Focus. Linnea Johnson-Scott left the Office of Support Enforcement late in 1992, but her successor, Jim Stroud, plans to continue her work, reaching out to young fathers as people with problems instead of as deadbeats and criminals. Ed

Woodley left Project MISTER also in late 1992 to start up The Bridge Program, which tries to address the needs of teenagers and young adults, both parents and nonparents.

Our Place in Evanston, Illinois, and the combined efforts of the Project MISTER and the Office of Support Enforcement in Washington State show how successful programs can be when they:

- use a range of strategies for getting young fathers involved;
- attract counselors and coordinators who use creativity to keep the young men interested and focused on positive goals
- demonstrate enough success with their programs that government agencies, community groups and ordinary citizens keep the programs going.

9

TAKING
RESPONSIBILITY

I [always] thought if I worked real hard I could make it, I could get ahead and be sole provider for my kids. . . . But when child support got me and they started taking practically all of my check . . . it was like this cloud came over my mentality. . . .

I got a job moving boxes. . . . The pay ain't that good, but I don't care . . . I ain't gonna stretch myself too far for the government.[1]

—A young father in Public/Private Ventures'
Young Unwed Fathers Pilot Project

It is always difficult to predict the future, about teenage fathers or anything else. One prediction about teenage fathers seems fairly safe, though: programs such as those described in the last chapter can only have a limited impact on the lives of the young dads and their children unless larger trends in society start to favor them. For instance:

• **Governmental policies and the economic health of the country** play huge roles in determining whether young fathers who want to help out their baby and its mother financially and who stick with education or job training will eventually be able to find work that will pay enough so their good intentions can become a reality. Welfare reform could reverse the problem reflected in the quotation that begins this chapter and encourage teenage fathers to live with their child and its mother.

• **Society's attitudes toward teenage males,** often so negative or even hostile, will inevitably shape new laws and changes in social-service programs—for better or worse. These attitudes will also have an impact on whether we reach out to young fathers and encourage them to maintain contact with their children or only see the fathers as a threat to "family values" and give up on them as real fathers.

In this chapter we will first look at how political, economic, and social changes are affecting teenage fathers who want to take on the burdens and rewards of fatherhood (including the importance of President Clinton's movement toward "family values," the limited job opportunities for young fathers, and a "get-tough" attitude in the general public) and then look at one sixteen year old whose story raises the troubling question: "When, if ever, should we give up on helping a troubled teenage father take part in the raising of his child?"

THE SWING TOWARD
"FAMILY VALUES"

The election of Democratic president Bill Clinton in 1992 came after twelve years of Republican presidents (Ronald Reagan and George Bush) who cut many programs in education, employment training, and child welfare. Clinton pledged during the presidential campaign to put more money into programs like job training for young people, which could enable young fathers to get the skills they need for a job with a future, one that will help them support their child.

During his first year in office, Clinton signed the Youth Fair Chance Program, which distributed $50,000,000 toward helping the long-term unemployed up to age of thirty.[2]

In December 1993, Clinton's task force on welfare reform tried to strengthen the stability of relationships between young parents by making it easier for them to get welfare payments when the father was living with the mother and child. David T. Ellwood, a member of the task force, explained that the change was needed since "We don't want there to be incentives that favor single-parent families. . . . This is all in the context of promoting parental responsibility."[3] Critics immediately pointed out that people wanted the number of people on welfare *cut*, not expanded. Little has been heard about this proposal since and debate on welfare reform in the mid-1990s continues to concentrate on further limiting the number of people eligible to get benefits.

By 1994, the Clinton administration had taken up the

theme of "family values" which had been a controversial topic during the 1992 presidential campaign. For Republicans like Dan Quayle, vice president under President Bush, family values include an emphasis on the importance fathers can have to the well-being and success of the children they bring into the world but all too often abandon. Quayle gave a speech in San Francisco in 1992 in which he asserted that:

> *Marriage is probably the best antipoverty program of all. . . . Where there are no mature, responsible men around to teach boys how to be good men, gangs serve in their place.*
>
> *Bearing babies irresponsibly is, simply, wrong. Failing to support children one has fathered is wrong.*[4]

Most of the controversy about the speech at the time came about because Quayle went on to criticize the fictional title character in the television comedy "Murphy Brown," who he said "mock[ed] the importance of fathers by bearing a child alone, and calling it just another 'lifestyle choice.'"[5]

The Clinton campaign criticized Dan Quayle's 1992 speech, calling it uncaring toward single mothers and hypocritical because the Republicans didn't propose any concrete steps to make families more stable or to improve the lives of babies born to unwed parents. But by early 1994, Clinton was telling a junior-high-school audience that family values could be restored by showing the same sense of personal responsibility that Quayle had called for:

We've got to make a decision. Every one of you
have to make it. Is it right or wrong if you're a
boy to get some girl pregnant and then forget
about it? I think it's wrong.

    I think it's not only wrong for them. I think
it's wrong for you. It's something you pay for the
rest of your life. . . . [S]omewhere there's some child
out there you didn't take care of who's in terrible
shape because of something you didn't do.[6]

President Clinton gave a second speech in September
1994 that was even more impassioned about the unfair-
ness to a baby of being brought into the world where it
will only have one unprepared parent. After pointing out
that four out of every ten children in this country are born
to unwed mothers, Clinton went on to say:

[Americans are] raising a whole generation of
children who aren't sure they're the most impor-
tant person in the world to anybody. That is a
disaster. It is wrong. And someone has to say
again . . . "You shouldn't have a baby before
you're ready, and you shouldn't have a baby
when you're not married." I know not everybody's
going to be in a stable, traditional family. . . .
But we'd be better off if more people were.[7]

In November 1994, Republicans won control of both the
Senate and House of Representatives for the first time
since the 1940s, running on a platform, which hundreds of
them had signed, called a "Republican Contract with
America." Newt Gingrich, the new Republican Speaker

of the House, called the plan a "first step toward renewing American civilization."[8] Among its ten policy points, the Contract spells out a series of welfare reforms that would have a direct effect on teenage fathers, their partners and children.

A teenage father already sometimes feels shut out of his baby's life, fearing that a governmental social service agency could decide it wasn't in the baby's best interest to have its father around, especially if he wasn't married to the baby's mother. According to a report in *U.S. News & World Report*, the Republicans' basic approach is to deny welfare "benefits for unwed mothers under 18, or even 21. . . . If young women still have babies they can't support, let them depend on families, charities and even orphanages."[9]

What effect would this have on a young unmarried father who was still trying to get the skills he needed for a job to support his baby? It might be his worst nightmare come true: the mother of his child unable to get welfare payments to take care of the baby and the baby itself taken away from its parents.

President Clinton called it a "disaster" for young people to have children they aren't able to raise well. The Republican attempt at welfare reform may discourage unprepared teenagers from having children, but it may make things even more difficult for the young father deciding if he should—or even can—be a part of his child's life.

ECONOMIC REALITIES AND HARDENING PUBLIC ATTITUDES

The number of teenage "deadbeat dads" and those fathers who want to contribute to their child's future but can't is unlikely to decrease unless teenage parents are helped to get the basic skills needed to get and keep a job. And even with this training, a young father may not be able to compete in the job market if the economy is not growing fast enough. Even the most motivated teenage fathers—those who complete their education or receive up-to-date job training—may have trouble finding good positions for themselves in the near future.

Teenage fathers, like teenage mothers, often have to sacrifice completing their education when they become parents. This failure to succeed academically and graduate from school often makes teenage fathers unable to support their children financially. Lack of academic success is also a predictor for teen parenthood: a teenager without the basic skills of reading, writing, math, and problem-solving is *three times* as likely to become a teenage father as teens with those skills.[10]

A study from the mid-1980s found that a young man just out of his teens had only *four in ten* chances of being able to support a family of three above the poverty line.[11] Teenage men have an even harder time getting and keeping a job that could provide for a family of three.

The economic outlook for the *children* of young parents has been getting worse. An increasing number of children are living in households below the poverty line and most of these children are in single-parent families, according to a review of 1990 census statistics by the Center for the Study of Social Policy.[12] The children of teenage parents have the greatest chance to be in single-parent households and run the greatest risk of growing up poor.

Statistics like these indicate that teenage fathers, their partners, and their offspring need the help of social programs as much as any group in society. But there's growing opposition to rebuilding the programs that benefit the underprivileged that were cut during the previous decade. There is even less support for creating expensive new projects. Instead, many Americans favor "getting tough" with groups like welfare recipients (especially unwed mothers and their children), young lawbreakers, and men who fail to provide child support for their children. Many young fathers believe that the hand that is offered to them from a government or social-service agency is likely to be a slap of punishment, rather than a reaching-out to help.

While attitudes about teenage males may come from unfair stereotypes, they affect everything: a welfare policy that cuts payments to a mother living with the father; visitation privileges that are sometimes unfairly denied to unwed fathers; enforcement of child-support laws even for young dads who want to be involved with their children but cannot afford financial support.

LARRY'S STORY: "I'M ALWAYS TRYIN' TO DO MORE AND MORE"

Larry Hobbs was in his mid-teens when he found out his girlfriend of four years was pregnant. During her pregnancy, he started participating in a young-fathers program called Our Place in Evanston, Illinois (discussed in the last chapter). Larry's story is told in his own words in Daniel B. Frank's *Deep Blue Funk & Other Stories: Portraits of Teenage Parents* (1983). This chapter has focused on recent trends that affect the teenage father and the obstacles he faces *today* if he tries to take responsibility for his child. However, Larry's story portrays struggles that young fathers are still facing.

Larry's example also shows how important it is not to give up too soon on young men who may only need the opportunity and some encouragement to take on the responsibilities and the rewards of being a father. But the end of his story reminds us that even good intentions and the resources of Our Place may not be enough (or may come too late) to make a teenager like Larry into a good role model for his child and a caring partner to its mother.

By the time Larry Hobbs had turned fifteen, he had fallen into a "deep blue funk." He told a group of young fathers at Our Place that it was "a lot deeper than a funk. It goes way down deep. Down to the depths. . . . I had nothin' to do and no energy to do nothin'. . . . The only damn thing I felt like doin' was copping' some bad reefer and gettin' high and stayin' high."[13]

Larry's "blue funk" started after Larry got thrown out of school and quit his job, both in the same week, and both after arguments with white adults. Explaining how he left his job, he says, "I was sick and tired of working for some white man. Let the white man earn *my* respect, is what I thought. I was tired of being a nobody to them."[14]

Larry falls into a sort of numb indifference after he finds out that his girlfriend, Sherelle, is pregnant and he asks her mother to lend them the money so Sherelle can get an abortion. Sherelle's mother shoots back, "Where are you going to get the money to pay me back? You don't work, do you? 'Cause if you did, you'd have some money to pay for this. No sir, I don't trust you."[15]

Larry is devastated by this, since he and Sherelle have been going out for four years. It is when he has fallen to the bottom, suspended from school, out of work, his girlfriend pregnant, told that her mother doesn't trust him, thinking about nothing but staying high, that he first links up with the Our Place program for young fathers.

Nothing happens overnight, but by the time we meet Larry again, at another Our Place meeting, he is a changed man: he has been in the delivery room with Sherelle for the birth of his son Claude a few days earlier, and he is holding down two jobs. Larry's own explanation for this change is that when Sherelle's mother insulted him by saying she didn't trust him, "It was like I was set on fire. And I knew the only way to prevent myself from being burned even more was to get myself together and get responsible."[16]

Our Place provided him with a place to air out his problems among other guys going through the same experience, and to get the encouragement he needs to grow up and "get responsible." He tells the other young fathers and the group leader, Ed, that he still needs their help at figuring out what he should do and at learning to accept that he can't do everything he'd like to for his newborn son:

> That's just it, Ed. I need some help too, for my big bout. 'Cause I've got to be about the business of helpin' my little son have a good role model he can look up to. You know, for the guidance a child needs. I really want to provide for my little family; provide the green stuff and the love we need to survive in this world. . . .
>
> Sometimes it's like I'm already at the limit, man, But then again, I think if I were a good father, I'd be doin' more for my son. . . . How am I supposed to know when 'more' is enough. . . . How do I know when I'm doin' enough?[17]

106

Ed, the group leader, tells Larry to trust his own words ("I'm already at my limit") and assures him and the other young fathers that they're not failures because they can't accomplish everything at once:

> *There are just some things you can't do now*
> *but will later on, at some other point. . . . You*
> *know, in an odd way, bein' a new parent is sort of*
> *like being a child. It's all a part of a developing*
> *process. Like your son, for example. He's got to sit*
> *up before he can crawl and crawl before he can*
> *walk, and walk before he can run."[18]*

Five months later, we see Larry for the last time. Some of his initial excitement has disappeared: bills are mounting, Sherelle seems to spend most of her time with her girlfriends, and her mother doesn't like him to come by and see Sherelle and Claude. We learn that he has gotten mad at Sherelle and punched her in the jaw. Sherelle's mother calls the police and it is only Ed's interference that keeps Larry out of jail.

Many people would feel that after this kind of violence Sherelle is wrong to allow Larry anywhere near his son. But Larry hasn't stopped thinking about his child. Having grown up since an early age in a family without a father, Larry still hasn't given up. As he tells Daniel Frank, ". . . [T]hat's my deep fear, man, that, without that stable family relationship, with me a strong father, my son will grow up like me when I was a kid; all wild and unruly . . . hating and being a fighter. I really want something different for my son."[19]

Larry is still only sixteen when the book ends and he

still has a long way to go at controlling his temper before he can make a difference for his son, which he sincerely wants to do. Perhaps if someone had taken an interest in him *before* he became a father, he would have been better prepared to deal with his emotions and control his violent impulses. In any case, he was lucky that his town had a place called "Our Place" when he needed it and that people there weren't about to let him give up on himself.

CONCLUSION

The most hopeful sign for teenage fathers may be that when Our Place opened its first young-fathers' program in the 1970s, it was one of the first places that served teen fathers in the country. Today, there are dozens of groups, using a variety of techniques to make young fathers better fathers. (See the section "Where to Go for Further Information" at the end of this book for some of them.) Today, there are at least a few adults in virtually every state who have built up organizations that reach out to young fathers as individuals. By working with teen dads, these adults have changed thousands of lives—those of young fathers and mothers and of their children.

Given the right opportunities, many young fathers want to help support their child and to become involved in their child's upbringing. Unfortunately, many find nothing but obstacles in their way and no one willing to spend the time to give help in getting over them. Every time a young man gives up on the "system" and himself and just walks away, a child and its mother suffer, and ultimately, society pays the price.

Part of the responsibility for these social costs lies with the young father—and mother—themselves. Part of the responsibility, however, lies with the society in which a teenage father lives, a society that offers him criticism when he fails but little respect when he succeeds and demands obligations from him without providing him the means to meet them. The situation of teenage fathers can start to improve once their attitudes toward sexual responsibility and their duty to the children they father change. But the real breakthrough may not come about until society stops giving up on teen fathers as a lost cause and provides them with the chance to become real parents to their children.

WHERE TO GO FOR MORE INFORMATION

ORGANIZATIONS

Many local chapters of The Society for the Prevention of Cruelty to Children and The Urban League have programs for young people that include services for teenage fathers.

The following are some of the organizations that have resources available or ongoing programs for young fathers:

The Bridge Program, 4720 32nd Ave. S., P.O. Box 18525, Seattle, WA 98118

Family Focus, 310 S. Peoria St., Suite 401, Chicago, IL 60607.

Fatherhood Project, Families and Work Institute, 330 Seventh Ave., 14th Floor, New York, NY 10001.

INSIGHTS Teen Parent Program, 1811 N.E. 39th Ave., Portland, OR 97212.

MELD, 123 North 3rd St., Suite 507, Minneapolis, MN 55401.

National Institute for Responsible Fatherhood &

Family Development, 8555 Hough Ave., Cleveland, OH 44106.

National Organization on Adolescent Pregnancy and Parenting (NOAPP), 4421-A East-West Highway, Bethesda, MD 20814.

Public/Private Ventures, 2005 Market St., Suite 900, Philadelphia, PA 19103 (has developed coordinated programs offering counseling and instruction in basic skills, job readiness, and job training at sites in six cities: Cleveland, OH; Fresno, CA; Racine, WI; Phildelphia, PA; Annapolis, MD; and St. Petersburg, FL).

Washington [State] Alliance Concerned with School Age Parents (WACSAP), 2366 Eastlake Ave. E., #408, Seattle, WA 98102.

VIDEOS

"Flour Babies" (app. 50 minutes), originally broadcast as a CBS-TV *Schoolbreak Special*: Morton Garcia, CBS-TV, 7800 Beverly Blvd., Los Angeles, CA 90036.

"He's No Hero" (18 1/2 minutes): Intermedia, 1300 Dexter Ave. N., Seattle, WA 98109.

"Me, A Teen Father?" (13 minutes): Centron Films (CEN), 1621 West 9th, Lawrence, KS 66044.

"Schoolboy Father" (30 minutes): Martin Tahse Productions, Learning Corporation of America, 1980.

"You're in the Picture: Stories of Teen Dads" (23 minutes): Intermedia, 1300 Dexter Ave. N., Seattle, WA 98109.

SOURCE NOTES

CHAPTER 1

1. Bryan E. Robinson, *Teenage Fathers* (Lexington, MA: Lexington Books, 1988), p. 3.
2. Ibid.

CHAPTER 2

1. Bryan E. Robinson, *Teenage Fathers* (Lexington, MA: Lexington Books, 1988), p. 3.
2. Arthur B. Elster and Michael E. Lamb, eds., *Adolescent Fatherhood* (Hillsdale, NJ: Lawrence Erlbaum Associates, 1986), p. 44.
3. Katherine B. Oettinger and Elizabeth C. Mooney, *"Not My Daughter": Facing Up to Adolescent Pregnancy* (Englewood Cliffs, NJ: Prentice-Hall, Inc., 1979), pp. 1–2.
4. Steve Bogira, "Daddy-Boys: Adolescent Fathers: The Forgotten Half of the Teenage Pregnancy Problem," *Chicago Reader*, August 12, 1983.

5. Katrine Ames and Marcus Mabry, "Practicing the Safest Sex of All," *Newsweek*, January 20, 1992, p. 52.

6. Jane Gross, "Sex Educators for Young See New Virtue in Chastity," *The New York Times*, January 16, 1994, p. 19.

7. Ibid.

8. Irene Sege, "Stress on Absent Fathers Is Urged," *Boston Globe*, January 10, 1992, p. 3.

CHAPTER 3

1. Steve Bogira, "Daddy-Boys: Adolescent Fathers: The Forgotten Half of the Teenage Pregnancy Problem," *Chicago Reader*, August 12, 1983.

2. Douglas M. Teti and Michael E. Lamb, "Sex-Role Learning and Adolescent Fatherhood," in Arthur B. Elster and Michael E. Lamb, eds., *Adolescent Fatherhood* (Hillsdale, NJ: Lawrence Erlbaum Associates, Publishers), p. 24.

3. Ibid.

4. Ibid.

5. Bryan E. Robinson, *Teenage Fathers* (Lexington, MA: Lexington Books, 1988), p. 56.

6. Bryan E. Robinson and Robert L. Barret, *The Developing Father: Emerging Roles in Contemporary Society* (New York: The Guilford Press, 1986), p. 170.

7. Ibid, p. 171.

8. Marcia A. Redmond, "Attitudes of Adolescent Males Toward Adolescent Pregnancy and Fatherhood," *Family Relations*, August, 1985, p. 342.

9. Ibid.

10.Steve Bogira, "Daddy-Boys."
11.Ibid.

CHAPTER 4

1. Jack Heinowitz, *Pregnant Fathers: How Fathers Can Enjoy and Share the Experiences of Pregnancy and Childbirth* (Englewood Cliffs, NJ: Prentice-Hall, Inc., 1982), p. 37.
2. Ibid.
3. Ibid., p. 89.
4. Rae Grad et al., *The Father Book* (Washington, DC: Acropolis, 1981) p. 50.
5. Heinowitz, pp. 88–91.
6. Mary Achatz and Crystal A. MacAllum, *Young Unwed Fathers: Report from the Field* (Philadelphia, PA: Public/Private Ventures, Spring 1994), p. 87.
7. Ibid.

CHAPTER 5

1. Margaret A. Konn, "Child Support Enforcement and Young Unwed Fathers," in Jacqueline Smollar et al., *Young Unwed Fathers: Research Review, Policy Dilemmas and Options* (Washington, D.C., 1987), p. 21.
2. Bryan E. Robinson and Robert L. Barret, *The Developing Father: Emerging Roles in Contemporary Society* (New York: The Guilford Press, 1986), p. 178.
3. Bryan E. Robinson, *Teenage Fathers* (Lexington, MA: D.C. Heath and Company, 1988), p. 42.
4. William Raspberry, "Teaching Responsible Fatherhood," *The Washington Post*, April 27, 1992.

115

5. Ibid.

6. CBS *This Morning*, June 19, 1992.

CHAPTER 6

1. Bryan E. Robinson, *Teenage Fathers* (Lexington, MA: D.C. Heath and Company, 1988), p. 60.

2. Ibid, p. 61.

3. Ibid.

4. Arthur B. Elster and Leo Hendricks, "Stresses and Coping Strategies of Adolescent Fathers" in Arthur B. Elster and Michael E. Lamb, eds., *Adolescent Fatherhood* (Hillsdale, NJ: Lawrence Erlbaum Associates, 1986), p. 63.

5. William Marsiglio, "Adolescent Fathers in the United States: Their Initial Living Arrangements, Marital Experience and Educational Outcomes," *Family Planning Perspectives*, November-December, 1987, p. 240.

6. Ibid, p. 248.

7. Jeanne Warren Lindsay, *Teenage Marriage: Coping with Reality*, rev. ed. (Buena Park, CA: Morning Glory Press, 1988), p. 13.

8. Bryan E. Robinson and Robert L. Barret, *The Developing Father: Emerging Roles in Contemporary Society* (New York: The Guilford Press, 1986), p. 178.

9. Ibid.

10. Bryan E. Robinson, *Teenage Fathers*, pp. 42–43.

11. Jeanne Warren Lindsay, *Teenage Marriage*, p. 129.

12. Jeanne Warren Lindsay, *School-Age Parents: The Challenge of Three-Generation Living* (Buena Vista, CA: Morning Glory Press, 1990), p. 79.

13. Ibid, p. 43.

14. Marsiglio, p. 244.

15. Patricia Voydanoff and Brenda W. Donnelley, *Adolescent Sexuality and Pregnancy* (Newbury Park, CA: Sage Publications, 1990), p. 77.

16. Ibid, p. 78.

17. Jeanne Warren Lindsay, *School-Age Parents*, p. 74.

18. Karen Gravelle and Leslie Peterson, *Teenage Fathers* (New York: Julian Messner, 1992), pp. 72-3.

19. Janet Mason, "Bringing Up Teenage Fathers," *Life*, June 1984, p. 100.

CHAPTER 7

1. Armstrong, *Adolescent Males and Teen Pregnancy*, p. 2.

2. William Marsiglio, "Adolescent Fathers in the United States: Their Initial Living Arrangements, Marital Experience and Educational Outcomes," *Family Planning Perspectives*, November-December 1987, p. 240.

3. John Lewis McAdoo, "Changing Perspectives on the Role of the Black Father," in Phyllis Bronstein and Carolyn Pape Cowan, eds., *Fatherhood Today: Men's Changing Role in the Family* (New York: John Wiley & Sons, 1988), p. 83.

4. Linda Anderson Smith, "Black Adolescent Fathers," *Social Work*, May-June, 1988, p. 270.

5. Deidre Forbes, "Mixed Messages," *The Voice*, October 12, 1991.

6. Ed O.G & Da Bulldogs, "Be a Father to Your Child," *Life of a Kid in the Ghetto* (Barney & Fred Music; BMI), 1991. Permission to use lyrics from Ed O. G & Da

Bulldogs' raps has been kindly granted by Focus Business Management.

7. Alfredo Mirande, "Chicano Father: Traditional Perceptions and Current Realities," in Phyllis Bronstein and Carolyn Pape Cowan, eds., *Fatherhood Today: Men's Changing Role in the Family* (New York: John Wiley & Sons, 1988), p. 96.

8. Alfredo Mirande, p. 99.

9. Ibid.

10. Mercer L. Sullivan, "Ethnographic Research on Young Fathers and Parenting: Implications for Public Policy," in Jacqueline Smollar et al., *Young Unwed Fathers: Research Review, Policy Dilemmas and Options* (Washington, D.C., 1987), p. 23.

CHAPTER 8

1. Bryan E. Robinson, *Teenage Fathers* (Lexington, MA: D.C. Heath and Company, 1988), p. 108.

2. Ibid, p. 109.

3. David Van Biema, "Unprepared, Unwanted and Unwed, Adolescent Fathers Get a Helping Hand from Counselor Ron Johnson," *People Weekly*, December 1, 1986, p. 82.

4. M. Laurie Leitch and Anne M. Gonzalez, "Involving the Young Unwed Father in Pregnancy and Adoption Counseling," in Jacqueline Smollar et al., *Young Unwed Fathers: Research Review, Policy Dilemmas and Options* (Washington, D.C., 1987), p. 16.

5. Ibid.

6. Debra G. Klinman et al., "The Teen Father

Collaboration: A Demonstration and Research Model," in Arthur B. Elster and Michael E. Lamb, eds., *Adolescent Fatherhood* (Hillsdale, NJ: Lawrence Erlbaum Associates, 1986), p. 168.

7. Joelle Sander, "The Teen Father Collaboration: A National Research and Demonstration Project," in Jacqueline Smollar's *Young Unwed Fathers*, p. 8.

CHAPTER 9

1. "One Father's Story, *Public/Private Ventures News*, Summer 1994, p. 2.

2. George Hager, "Congress Clears Supplemental, Offsets Most of the Costs," *Congressional Quarterly Weekly Reports*, July 3, 1993, p. 1719.

3. Jason DeParle, "Welfare Plan Would Ease Aid to 2-Parent Homes," *New York Times*, December 10, 1993, p. A1.

4. Knight-Ritter Service, "'Moral Values': Some Passages from the Speech," *Boston Globe*, May 22, 1992, p. 17.

5. Ibid.

6. Gwen Ifill, "Clinton Warns Youths of Perils of Pregnancy," *New York Times*, February 4, 1994, p. A18.

7. Michael Wines, "Clinton Speech Stresses Issues of Morality," *New York Times*, September 10, 1994, p. 1.

8. *Facts on File*, September 29, 1994, p. 703.

9. Steven V. Roberts with Kenneth T. Walsh, "Squaring Off Over Values," *U.S. News & World Report*, November 28, 1994, p. 49.

10. Morton H. Sklar, "Employment and Training for

Unwed Fathers: An Unmet and Unrecognized Need," in Jacqueline Smollar et al., *Unwed Fathers: Research Review, Policy Dilemmas and Options* (Washington, D.C., 1987), p. 5.

11. Ibid.

12. "Pulse: Children and Poverty," *The New York Times*, November 9, 1992, p. B1.

13. Daniel B. Frank, *Deep Blue Funk & Other Stories: Portraits of Teenage Parents* (Chicago: The Ounce of Prevention Fund, 1983), p. 151.

14. Ibid, p. 156.

15. Ibid, p. 159.

16. Ibid.

17. Ibid, pp. 178–9.

18. Ibid, pp. 179–80.

19. Ibid, pp. 190–1.

FOR FURTHER READING

BOOKS

Ayer, Eleanor, H. *Everything You Need to Know About Teen Fatherhood*. New York: The Rosen Publishing Group, Inc., 1993 (the easiest-to-read nonfiction book for teenage fathers; well illustrated).

Frank, Daniel B. *Deep Blue Funk & Other Stories: Portraits of Teenage Parents*, Chicago, IL: The Ounce of Prevention Fund, 1983. (The stories of teenagers who took part in programs at Our Place in Evanston, IL, in large part told in their own words. The chapter "Deep Blue Funk," pp. 151–92, portrays a young fathers group. A half-hour play based on four young parents portrayed in the book—including one teen father—is available from Dramatic Publishing Company.)

Gravelle, Karen, and Leslie Peterson. *Teenage Fathers*, Englewood Cliffs, NJ: Julian Messner, 1992 (interviews with thirteen teenage fathers).

Lindsay, Jeanne Warren. *Teenage Dads: Rights, Responsibilities and Joys*. Buena Park, CA: Morning Glory

Press, 1993 (an excellent "how-to" book for young fathers: a teaching guide to the book is also available for instructors).

———*School-Age Parents: The Challenge of Three Generation Living*. Buena Park, CA: Morning Glory Press, 1990.

——— *Teenage Marriage: Coping with Reality*. Buena Park, CA: Morning Glory Press, 1988.

——— *Teens Parenting: The Challenge of Babies and Toddlers*. Buena Park, CA: Morning Glory Press, 1981.

Robinson, Bryan E. *Teenage Fathers*. Lexington, MA: D.C. Heath and Company, 1988 (advanced reading level; probably the best adult overview of young fathers).

Woodbury, Marda, and Donna L. Richardson, eds. *Youth Information Resources*. New York: Greenwood Press, 1987 (extensive guide to services for children and teenagers; includes names, addresses, phone and sometimes fax and on-line access numbers for many organizations and resources for the teen father).

ARTICLES

[Author not given], "Teen Dads Get Attention, Too," *NEA Today*, March 1994, p. 7.

Colt, George Howe. "Children with Children," *Life*, July 1991, pp. 78–89.

Gregory, Sophronia Scott. "Teaching Young Fathers the Ropes," *Time*, August 10, 1992, p. 49.

Larner, Jeremy. "The Sins of Our Fathers: Robin Jackson Turns Angry Young Men into Proud Parents," *Esquire*, December 1984, pp. 264–67.

Mason, Janet. "Bringing Up Teenage Fathers," *Life*, June 1984, pp. 96–104.

Robinson, Bryan E., and Robert L. Barret. "Teenage Fathers," *Psychology Today*, December 1985, pp. 66–70.

Thomas, Evan et al. "The Reluctant Father," *Newsweek*, December 19, 1988, pp. 64–66.

Whitman, David. "A Father's Place in the Welfare State: Men Need Not Be the Forgotten Partners in Bringing Up Baby," *U.S. News & World Report*, October 17, 1988, pp. 41 and 44.

INDEX